MW00812194

NUMBERING IN AMERICAN SIGN LANGUAGE

Brenda E. Cartwright and Suellen J. Bahleda

RID Press

RID Press
Registry of Interpreters for the Deaf
333 Commerce St, Alexandria, VA 22314
703.838.0030 (V), 703.838.0454 (FAX), 703.838.0459 (TTY)
www.rid.org

Registry of Interpreters for the Deaf

RID is a national membership organization representing the professionals who facilitate communication between people who are deaf or hard of hearing and people who can hear. Established in 1964 and incorporated in 1974, RID is a tax-exempt 501(c)(3) nonprofit organization.

It is the mission of RID to provide international, national, regional, state and local forums and an organizational structure for the continued growth and development of the profession of interpretation and transliteration of American Sign Language and English.

RID Press is the professional publishing arm of RID. The mission of RID Press is to extend the reach and reputation of RID through the publication of scholarly, practical, artistic and educational materials that advance the learning and knowledge of the profession of interpreting. The Press seeks to reflect the mission of RID by publishing a wide range of works that promote recognition and respect for the language and culture of deaf people and the practitioners in the field.

RID Press is a division of the Registry of Interpreters for the Deaf, 333 Commerce St, Alexandria, VA 22314, USA, (703) 838-0030, (703) 838-0459 TTY, www.rid.org

Published 2003

Library of Congress Control Number: 2002115164

Amazon ISBN 9780916883126

Printed in the United States of America

Contents

Authors' Note vii

Introduction ix

■ Unit One: Numbers 0–99 1
- Preventing Repetitive Motion Injuries 2
- Overview 3
- Drill Practice Goals 6
- Drill: Numbers 0–99 7
- Activities: Things on the Tube 8
  - Around the Room 9
  - 100 on the Dot 10

■ Unit Two: Hundreds 11
- Warm-Up Exercises 12
- Overview 13
- Drills: Hundreds 14
  - More Hundreds 15
  - Hundreds Incorporating Teens and Twenties 16
- Activities: Dewey Decimal Game 17
  - Let's Get Personal 19

■ Unit Three: Thousands, Millions, and Billions 21
- Warm-Up Exercises 22
- Overview 23
- Drills: Thousands 25
  - Tens of Thousands 26
  - Hundreds of Thousands, Millions, and Billions 27
- Activities: Points of Light Shelter Statistics 28
  - Population of the World's Largest Cities 29
  - The Greatest Show on Earth 30
  - Telephone Game 31

■ Unit Four: Telephone Numbers, Addresses, Zip Codes, and Social Security Numbers 33
- Warm-Up Exercises 34
- Overview 35
- Drills: Telephone Numbers 36
  - Zip Codes 37
- Activities: Business Cards 38
  - How Far? 39
  - Dewey Decimal Game 40
  - Number Relay 42

■ Unit Five: Time and Age	**43**
Warm-Up Exercises	44
Overview	45
Drill: Time	46
Activities: Don't Miss the Bus!	47
Numbers Are from Venus and Mars and . . .	49
Day Planner	50
Planner	51
■ Unit Six: Time Measurement	**53**
Warm-Up Exercises	54
Overview	55
Activities: How Long Does It Take?	56
Let's Get Personal	58
Getting Creative	59
Number Relay	60
■ Unit Seven: Decades and Centuries	**61**
Warm-Up Exercises	62
Overview	63
Drills: Years	64
Activities: They Lived, They Died	65
100 Freestyle Olympic Champions	66
School District Enrollment	67
Average SAT Test Scores	69
■ Unit Eight: Money and Percents	**71**
Warm-Up Exercises	72
Overview	73
Activities: Here's a Tip	74
Home Prices in the USA	75
Let's Buy a House	76
Meal-Lodging Cost Index	77
Getting Creative	79
Let's Make a Car Deal	80
Vegetarian Restaurant	81
Shopping Trends	82
Do the Math	83
■ Unit Nine: Pronouns, Height, and Measurement	**85**
Warm-Up Exercises	86
Overview	87
Activities: All about Animals	88
Big and Small	89
Let's Get Personal	90
Hot, Cold, Rain, Snow	91
Favorite Recipes	92
Calorie and Fat Content	94
Women's Basketball	95

■ **Unit Ten: Fractions** 97
Warm-Up Exercises 98
Overview 99
Activities: Food for Thought 100
Investor's Diary 101
When in Rome, or Paris, or Rio . . . 102
Telephone Game 103

■ **Unit Eleven: Ordinal Numbers** 105
Warm-Up Exercises 106
Overview 107
Activities: Take Me out to the Ballgame 108
Peanuts & Crackerjacks 109
Major League Baseball 110
Let's Get Personal 111
Out to Lunch 112
Dewey Decimal Game 113

■ **Unit Twelve: Numbers in Sports** 115
Warm-Up Exercises 116
Overview 117
Activities: Sports Scores 118
At the Track: Horse Racing 119
Getting Creative 120
Number Relay 121

Appendix A: Numbers 0–10 Illustrations 123

Bibliography and Resource List 125

Authors' Note

This book is the result of more than ten years of development, experimentation, and collaboration. Instructional approaches to counting and numeric incorporation have evolved over time with additional linguistic knowledge and insights into American Sign Language (ASL). This text has grown out of our need, as faculty members of ASL and interpreter programs, to better incorporate numbering systems into our curricula.

These instructional materials include drills and expressive and receptive activities. Our goal was to create a practical, useful, and comprehensive approach to teaching numbers and their variations across applications in ASL. The process of developing this text energized us and challenged us to evaluate our own instructional approaches and materials. We believe this book and its companion book, *Fingerspelling in American Sign Language,* capture that energy and will enhance numbering instruction across the spectrum, from beginning students to interpreters-in-training.

Our thanks to Deaf artist Mary Klein, who contributed the illustrations for this book. In addition, our gratitude and appreciation goes out to students, workshop participants, and esteemed colleagues who provided testing grounds and invaluable feedback over the years.

Brenda E. Cartwright, MS
CSC, CI and CT
Lansing Community College
Lansing, Michigan
BCartwright@lcc.edu

Suellen J. Bahleda, M.ED, M.DIV
CI and CT
University of Alaska Anchorage
Anchorage, Alaska
rwpress@juno.com

Introduction

Learning to count is just the beginning of using numbering systems within ASL. Incorporating a wide range of numbering uses into practice is critical for your linguistic development. This text provides an informative, positive, and practical approach to numbering practice to help you learn numbering as an integral part of ASL, rather than an isolated component.

Your initial exposure to numbering and numbering systems, and how you incorporate numbers into practice, can greatly impact your attitude and ability to successfully use numbers in your own signing. This book provides a positive framework for learning numbering systems, with information and activities (expressive and receptive) for meaningful and fun practice.

Unit One: Numbers 0–99

- Preventing Repetitive Motion Injuries
- Overview
- Drill Practice Goals
- Drill: Numbers 0–99
- Activities: Things on the Tube
  Around the Room
  100 on the Dot

Preventing Repetitive Motion Injuries

ASL and interpreter programs can play an important role in preventing repetitive motion injuries (Stewart et al., 1988). Just as athletes warm up and increase their stamina in increments, so should signers and interpreters. You are encouraged to do warm-up stretches before numbering practice.

The following warm-up stretches can reduce the amount of stress the hand, wrist, arm, and shoulder receive while fingerspelling and signing. Each class session should begin with a variety of warm ups to limit potential cumulative trauma disorders. Warm-up stretches may be selected from the following:

Warm-Up Exercises

Shoulder Shrugs: Slowly raise and drop shoulders several times.

The Swan Dive: Slowly stretch arms above your head until they meet, palms together. Gently lower them to shoulder level, palms up. Repeat.

Finger Lifts: Place hand palm down on a table or flat surface and slowly raise and lower each finger. Repeat with the other hand.

Full Arm Stretch: Hold arm out parallel to the floor, palm down. Lock elbow. Raise your hand so the fingertips point to the ceiling. With the other hand, gently press the raised fingers back toward your body for a five-count. Alternate with the other hand. Repeat twice.

Palm Press: Press palms together in front of your body. Keeping your elbows high, use the right palm to gently and slowly push the left palm backwards, from the wrist only, toward the left elbow. Slowly and gently, use the left palm to push the right palm backwards, from the wrist only, toward the right elbow. Repeat several times.

The Frankenstein: With arms stretched out in front of you, palms down, slowly open and close hands, stretching the fingers apart as far as possible. Repeat several times.

Wrist Revolutions: With closed hands, slowly rotate wrists in toward each other several times. Then rotate wrists away from each other several times.

Overview

Numbers 0–9

The palm faces out for 0, in for numbers 1–5, and out for 6–9 (see Appendix A). However, the palm faces out for 1–5 when they are in the "ones" position of a larger number (32, 64, 275, etc.).

Numbers 16–19

There are variations for signing 16–19, although the most common method used is a combination sign: start with the "10" handshape (do not shake) and twist outward to the 6–9 position (10 + 6 = 16, 10 + 7 = 17, etc.).

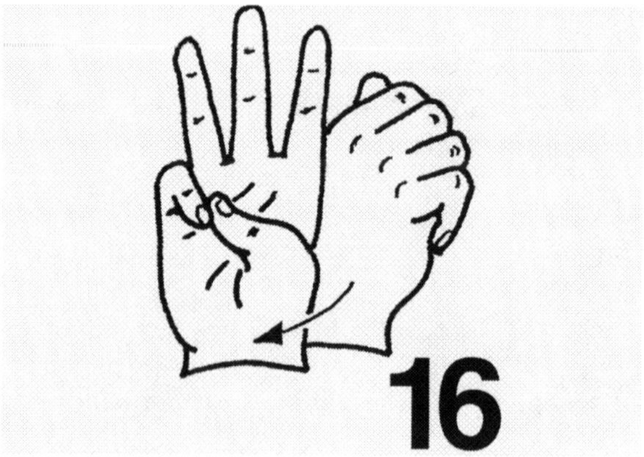

Decade Numbers

There is a specific sign for 20, while other "decade" numbers (30, 50, 80, etc.) are made by signing 3 + 0, 5 + 0, 8 + 0, and so on.

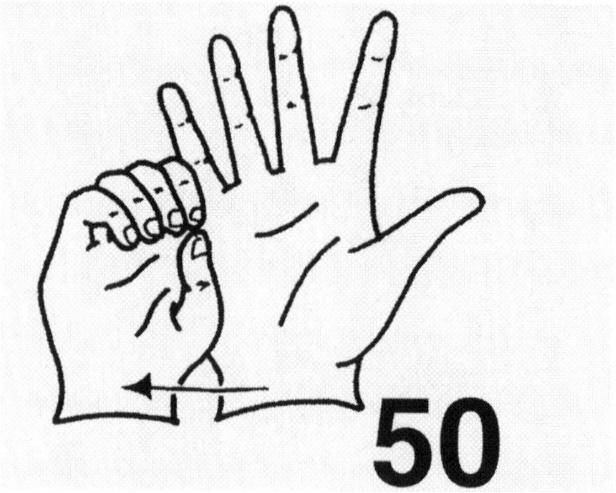

Double Numbers

Double numbers (22, 33, 55, 77) are produced with the palm down, parallel to the floor. The number taps twice, moving from the center of the body out to the dominant side.

Numbers 21–29

These numbers (except 22) use an "L" shape as the root, rather than the handshape "2."

Numbers 23 and 25

These numbers have variants. They can be produced following the pattern described above (the "L" root + 3, the "L" root +5). A variant for 23 is to produce the number 3, palm out, and wiggle the middle finger. For 25, produce the number 5, palm out, and wiggle either the middle finger or both the middle finger and ring finger together.

Numbers 67–69, 76–79 (excluding 77), 86–89 (excluding 88), and 96–98

These numbers incorporate specific movements for clarity. When the "tens" number is smaller than the "ones" (67, 78, 89), the first number is made away from the body, and the second number rocks toward the center of the body. When the "tens" number is larger than the "ones" (76, 86, 98), the first number is made at the center of the body, and the second number rocks away from the body.

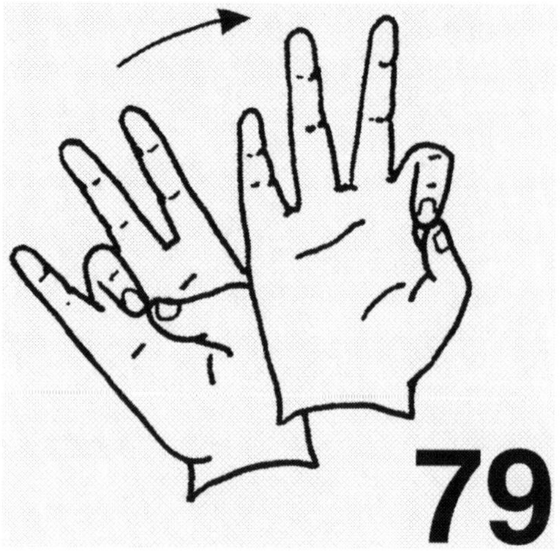

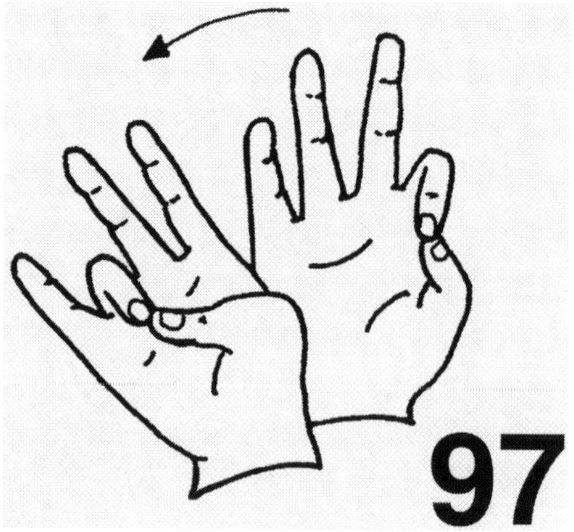

Drill Practice Goals

Numbering drills meet a number of practice goals:

- Drills are used to build up and increase stamina. Focused practice on numbering can be physically demanding. Students should do warm-up exercises before beginning numbering practice.
- Drills reinforce production of numbers as a whole within a context, rather than as a number-by-number string.
- Drills reinforce the differences in numbering production based on context.
- Drills assist in the development of rhythm and cadence.

Drill: Numbers 0–99

54	15	80	63
78	24	8	89
96	49	92	50
99	82	53	44
35	87	36	81
88	83	1	41
59	2	67	62
6	79	16	69
55	10	70	21
64	97	7	72
11	75	73	27
18	76	26	68
77	23	25	61
22	57	14	20
71	60	5	19
66	29	56	12
17	52	9	84
90	33	38	98
51	47	45	48
91	86	37	85
94	43	3	32
42	0	46	39
58	74	28	13
30	65	4	93
95	31	34	40

Things on the Tube

> **Suggested Activity:** Using the TV schedule provided below, answer the following questions:

1. What channel will "Friends" be on this Saturday?
2. What channel will "The Simpsons" be on this Sunday?
3. What channel will "General Hospital" be on this Saturday?
4. What channel will "Boston Public" be on this Sunday?
5. What channel will "The Practice" be on this Sunday?
6. What channel will "Frasier" be on this Saturday?
7. What channel will "Ally McBeal" be on this Saturday?
8. What channel will "Will & Grace" be on this Sunday?
9. What channel will "ER" be on this Saturday?
10. What channel will "The Young and the Restless" be on this Sunday?

SATURDAY		
Time	**Channel**	**Program**
11:00 a.m.	4	As The World Turns
3:00p.m.	6	General Hospital
4:00p.m.	5	Frasier
6:30p.m.	8	ER
8:00p.m.	7	Ally McBeal
10:00 p.m.	9	Friends
SUNDAY		
Time	**Channel**	**Program**
10:00 a.m.	9	The Young and the Restless
1:30p.m.	3	Guiding Light
2:00p.m.	4	The Simpsons
2:30p.m.	6	Boston Public
5:00p.m.	2	Will & Grace
7:30p.m.	5	The Practice

Around the Room

> **Suggested Activity:** In a group, have the first person sign 1, the second person sign 2, etc., up to 100. Then repeat the activity, going backwards; the first person signs 100, the second person signs 99, etc.

100 on the Dot

> **Suggested Activity:** Arrange seats in a circle. Decide who will go first. That student chooses a number between 1 and 10, and signs it. The next student chooses a number between 1 and 10 and adds to the first student's number, signing the sum. This continues around the circle, with each person signing the new sum, until one person can add a number that makes 100 . . . on the dot.

Unit Two: Hundreds

- Warm-Up Exercises
- Overview
- Drills: Hundreds
More Hundreds
Hundreds Incorporating Teens and Twenties
- Activities: Dewey Decimal Game
Let's Get Personal

Warm-Up Exercises

Shoulder Shrugs: Slowly raise and drop shoulders several times.

The Swan Dive: Slowly stretch arms above your head until they meet, palms together. Gently lower them to shoulder level, palms up. Repeat.

Finger Lifts: Place hand palm down on a table or flat surface and slowly raise and lower each finger. Repeat with the other hand.

Full Arm Stretch: Hold arm out parallel to the floor, palm down. Lock elbow. Raise your hand so the fingertips point to the ceiling. With the other hand, gently press the raised fingers back toward your body for a five-count. Alternate with the other hand. Repeat twice.

Palm Press: Press palms together in front of your body. Keeping your elbows high, use the right palm to gently and slowly push the left palm backwards, from the wrist only, toward the left elbow. Slowly and gently, use the left palm to push the right palm backwards, from the wrist only, toward the right elbow. Repeat several times.

The Frankenstein: With arms stretched out in front of you, palms down, slowly open and close hands, stretching the fingers apart as far as possible. Repeat several times.

Wrist Revolutions: With closed hands, slowly rotate wrists in toward each other several times. Then rotate wrists away from each other several times.

Overview

Hundreds

The formal sign for 100, 200, 300, . . . 900, is 1 + C, 2 + C, 3 + C, . . . 9 + C.

A typical variant for 100–500 is created by forming a representation of the "C" with only the number sign involved. Therefore, 400 would be made by signing 4 and then crooking/bending those four fingers, still separated, and pulling back slightly.

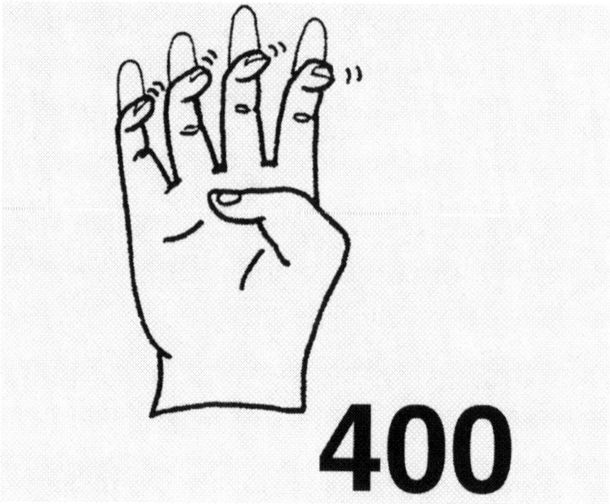

Note: This variant can be used as a stand-alone for 200–500, but not for 100. 100 is signed 1 + C, but once additional numbers are incorporated (e.g., 101, 156, 188), the variant can be employed. This variant can only be used for 100–500; the numbers 600–900 must be signed 6 + C, 7 + C, 8 + C, and 9 + C.

Drill: Hundreds

642	369	825	901
753	470	936	112
147	223	975	692
258	334	186	703
362	445	297	814
470	556	308	925
581	667	419	136
692	778	521	247
713	889	632	358
864	581	824	991
743	469	935	112
398	915	580	667
844	561	145	212
388	951	589	656
176	793	368	445
409	126	691	778
166	783	367	434
854	571	146	222
511	237	712	889
612	348	822	989
955	672	256	323
287	804	479	556
733	459	934	101
277	894	478	545
501	237	711	878
622	348	823	990
499	126	690	767
965	682	247	334
279	422	858	640
225	123	169	459
323	592	812	947
460	325	876	423
561	477	835	793
723	935	317	167
851	512	137	682

Drill: More Hundreds

527	671	148	160
849	915	460	782
383	271	804	494
848	961	459	582
627	738	248	359
283	382	704	893
850	272	471	793
161	472	682	950
515	959	126	405
493	737	904	348
394	504	815	516
638	259	749	172
360	926	693	115
137	212	577	994
454	225	836	318
421	167	991	624
381	535	232	723
341	248	174	825
491	223	823	270
623	281	375	541
592	693	911	625
157	227	587	615
320	158	392	268
627	348	237	153
298	125	804	425
726	310	575	999
699	755	133	722
866	244	843	466
155	299	577	933
688	322	344	677
366	533	899	855
744	888	488	922
977	799	566	444
522	166	877	433
355	788	933	766

Drill: Hundreds Incorporating Teens and Twenties

215	321	419	528
618	727	316	422
520	629	719	828
417	523	621	711
820	929	518	624
722	812	921	111
619	725	823	913
122	212	720	826
924	114	223	313
821	927	125	215
324	414	922	128
226	316	425	515
123	229	327	417
526	616	224	320
428	518	627	717
325	421	529	619
728	818	426	522
611	720	829	919
527	623	712	821
911	120	628	724
813	922	112	221
729	825	914	123
213	322	811	926
115	224	314	423
912	127	216	325
415	524	113	228
317	426	516	625
214	329	418	527
617	726	315	411
519	628	718	827
416	512	620	729
819	928	517	613
721	811	920	129
618	714	822	912
121	211	719	815

Dewey Decimal Game

> **Suggested Activity:** Divide into pairs. Each student takes a different list of Dewey Decimal System numbers for a variety of topics. Ask and answer the following questions using the tables below.

1. What do I consider when buying a camera?
2. Where can I find a Farmer's Almanac?
3. I need a book about Michelangelo.
4. Where can I find a copy of the Chicago Tribune?
5. How do you keep score in baseball?
6. I need a copy of Outdoor Life.
7. Where can I find an Italian dictionary?
8. Are there any books about The Beatles?
9. Where can I find a book about the famous architect Frank Lloyd Wright?
10. Where can I find books about the Protestant Reformation?

Dewey Decimal System

000	COMPUTERS, INTERNET & SYSTEMS	**400**	LANGUAGE
010	Bibliographies	410	Linguistics
020	Library & information science	420	English & Old English languages
030	Encyclopedias & books of facts	430	German & related languages
040	[Unassigned]	440	French & related languages
050	Magazines, journals, and serials	450	Italian, Romanian & related languages
060	Associations, organizations, & museums	460	Spanish & Portuguese languages
070	Journalism, publishing & news media	470	Latin & Italic languages
080	Quotations	480	Classical & modern Greek languages
090	Manuscripts and rare books	490	Other Languages

Dewey DecimalSystem—cont'd

200	RELIGION	700	ARTS
210	Philosophy & theory of religion	710	Landscaping & area planning
220	The Bible	720	Architecture
230	Christianity & Christian theology	730	Sculpture, ceramics, & metalworks
240	Christian practice and observance	740	Drawing & decorative arts
250	Christian pastoral practice and religious orders	750	Painting
260	Church organization, social work & worship	760	Graphic arts
270	History of Christianity	770	Photography
280	Christian denominations	780	Music
290	Other religions	790	Sports, games & entertainment

Let's Get Personal

> **Suggested Activity:** With a partner, share the following numerical information (real or invented). Be sure to use appropriate ASL structure and grammatical features.

1. Me:
    - Age?
    - Birthdate?
    - Social security number?
    - Phone number?

2. My Family:
    - Parents' ages?
    - Siblings' ages?
    - Number of pets?
    - Number of children?

3. Food:
    - Number of times you eat out per week?
    - Slices of pizza usually consumed in one sitting?
    - Number of canned/bottled carbonated beverages you drink per week?
    - Daily calorie intake?

4. Intimate Details:
    - How many times per day do you brush your teeth?
    - How many bottles of cologne or perfume do you have?
    - How many pairs of shoes do you own?
    - How many pictures of family and friends do you have in your wallet?

Unit Three: Thousands, Millions, and Billions

- **Warm-Up Exercises**
- **Overview**
- **Drills: Thousands**
  Tens of Thousands
  Hundreds of Thousands, Millions, and Billions
- **Activities: Points of Light Shelter Statistics**
  Population of the World's Largest Cities
  The Greatest Show on Earth
  Telephone Game

Warm-Up Exercises

Shoulder Shrugs: Slowly raise and drop shoulders several times.

The Swan Dive: Slowly stretch arms above your head until they meet, palms together. Gently lower them to shoulder level, palms up. Repeat.

Finger Lifts: Place hand palm down on a table or flat surface and slowly raise and lower each finger. Repeat with the other hand.

Full Arm Stretch: Hold arm out parallel to the floor, palm down. Lock elbow. Raise your hand so the fingertips point to the ceiling. With the other hand, gently press the raised fingers back toward your body for a five-count. Alternate with the other hand. Repeat twice.

Palm Press: Press palms together in front of your body. Keeping your elbows high, use the right palm to gently and slowly push the left palm backwards, from the wrist only, toward the left elbow. Slowly and gently, use the left palm to push the right palm backwards, from the wrist only, toward the right elbow. Repeat several times.

The Frankenstein: With arms stretched out in front of you, palms down, slowly open and close hands, stretching the fingers apart as far as possible. Repeat several times.

Wrist Revolutions: With closed hands, slowly rotate wrists in toward each other several times. Then rotate wrists away from each other several times.

Overview

Thousands

THOUSAND issigned:

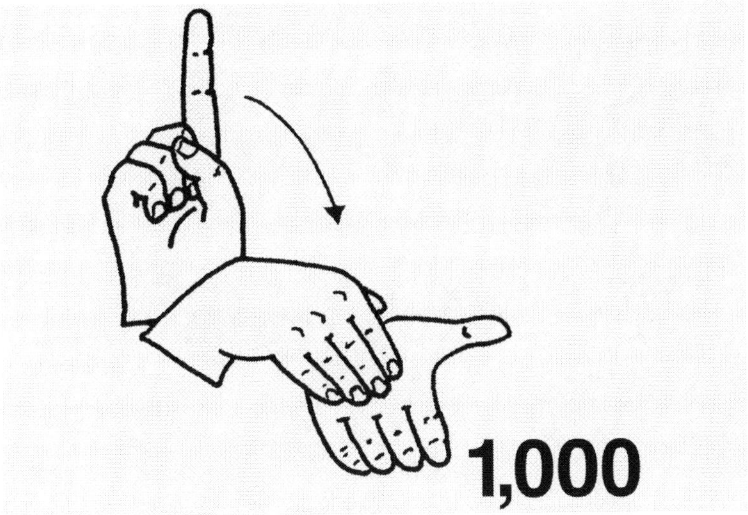

When the numbers 1–5 are in the "thousands" position, the palm faces out. For example, in the numbers 2,879 and 4,690, the 2 and the 4 will face out.

Numbers above 999 should be signed reflecting their decimal placements and grouping; 321,615 would be signed as THREE-HUNDRED TWENTY-ONE THOUSAND SIX-HUNDRED FIFTEEN.

Additionally, although a number like 1,500 may be spoken as "fifteen hundred," ASL would generally convert it to ONE THOUSAND FIVE HUNDRED.

Millions

MILLION issigned

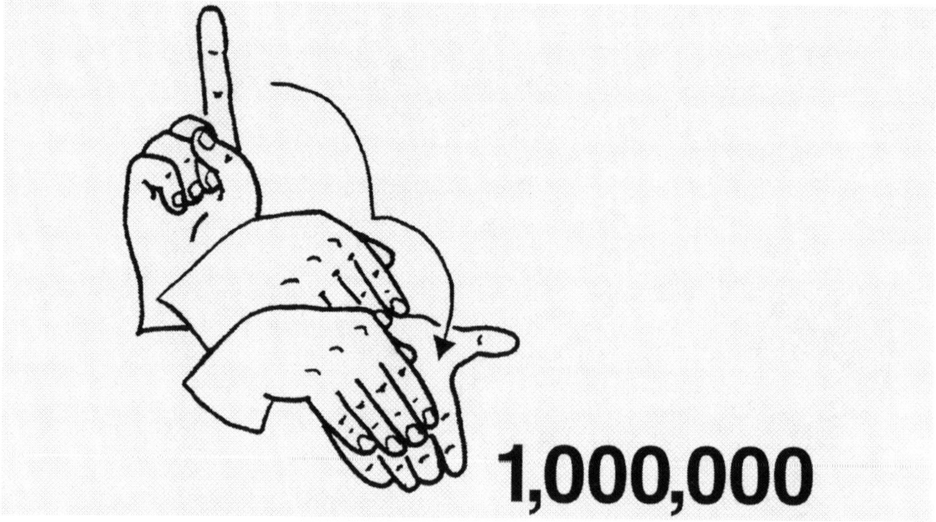

Billions andTrillions

The words "billion" and "trillion" are fingerspelled.

Drill: Thousands

1,655	8,322	2,744	5,077
4,966	9,411	3,877	4,988
3,855	1,633	9,433	8,300
2,866	3,611	6,344	1,499
6,188	5,099	4,722	2,500

5,833	7,111	8,566	9,277
1,244	9,099	3,255	5,611
3,488	9,144	7,622	8,233
2,366	4,388	6,477	4,688
6,533	1,777	1,066	5,599

4,522	7,355	2,199	2,844
3,766	6,733	8,977	7,855
7,518	1,317	4,816	5,655
8,015	4,911	2,222	7,032
5,917	2,207	1,829	2,540

3,506	1,123	6,319	3,316
7,510	4,031	1,321	2,184
1,700	3,636	1,972	8,119
6,363	9,461	1,050	7,639
2,211	4,414	8,123	3,431

2,690	1,741	7,207	5,539
6,496	4,273	8,585	2,716
8,251	3,359	6,044	4,228
4,298	2,965	8,579	4,042
7,311	6,202	1,854	5,309

2,864	9,531	5,113	3,076
6,410	3,935	1,642	7,480
9,743	4,187	8,426	3,864
4,975	2,753	1,757	9,668
6,399	7,521	5,298	8,632

3,016	9,405	4,278	8,823
5,430	7,611	6,651	6,430
7,893	5,258	8,025	1,489
1,789	6,239	9,101	6,066
4,834	3,906	1,238	1,568

Drill: Tens of Thousands

20,315	12,168	48,711	62,397
63,336	45,505	97,725	25,416
25,173	90,628	67,531	64,208
36,284	89,517	78,642	53,197
12,840	76,420	13,951	47,395

90,864	79,515	32,086	66,420
81,739	22,608	45,173	80,628
44,208	35,173	92,840	33,719
70,628	56,284	31,975	68,406
44,714	22,936	55,825	71,322

77,047	69,433	44,592	66,933
88,158	55,603	58,544	44,377
22,545	61,477	66,989	88,111
27,733	99,434	77,090	12,822
99,211	66,101	97,888	55,665

77,212	44,554	55,807	23,466
33,481	28,955	99,269	52,599
11,222	17,233	46,577	22,370
37,055	88,323	33,656	97,844
22,322	33,066	18,399	44,913

14,677	23,799	33,433	70,277
11,579	24,062	91,739	65,319
69,517	87,531	23,951	46,284
88,642	42,017	20,810	77,531
34,711	58,406	10,844	42,218

70,835	11,946	91,153	45,389
75,380	34,279	90,264	55,719
56,498	39,724	92,057	20,835
81,946	78,486	48,613	66,491
12,057	64,820	23,168	57,502

Drill: Hundreds of Thousands, Millions, and Billions

137,508	916,886	785,873	446,439
572,942	349,139	118,166	992,985
896,984	452,520	683,153	248,619
335,328	113,494	557,549	127,997
359,720	238,308	563,651	794,664
779,767	907,095	461,831	828,522
805,913	674,762	229,217	668,658
392,036	727,713	148,411	660,489
426,253	901,955	843,581	365,669
993,126	359,580	935,692	484,147
515,174	328,873	819,834	576,258
282,247	704,095	296,752	337,332
668,369	474,748	852,510	692,976
175,631	583,827	751,470	471,368
965,391	629,357	398,024	510,246
1,641,423	4,092,138	6,528,630	2,475,397
3,359,569	5,142,940	9,237,681	7,348,754
8,300,875	1,658,638	2,775,107	9,492,982
5,944,406	1,506,215	3,142,203	2,035,837
8,378,431	9,962,527	4,531,632	9,885,607
65,324,467	40,579,021	22,911,688	93,849,770
10,439,895	23,103,684	44,208,765	30,161,633
90,454,975	14,894,722	26,021,668	88,233,864
42,783,277	78,931,854	40,767,111	92,677,313
54,303,855	64,305,115	38,946,399	76,119,427
136,046,935,815	258,281,629,803	7,470,425,069	27,357,045,839
9,273,361,769	26,338,414,957	5,182,597,148	47,286,037,136
119,259,583,991	48,247,181,626	94,036,171,471	8,162,148,703
70,051,583,969	4,624,712,259	12,823,555,477	13,657,412,883

Points of Light Shelter Statistics

> **Suggested Activity:** With a partner, ask and answer the questions below using the table provided.

1. How many people were served in April 1998? November 1999?
2. Monthly average of people served in 1998?
3. Total number of people served in 2001?
4. Lowest number of people served in 1999?
5. Highest number of people served in 2000?
6. How many people were served in October 1998?
7. Monthly average of people served in 1999?
8. How many people were served in August 1998? August 1999? August 2000? August 2001?
9. Total number of people served in 2000?
10. How many people were served in May 2001?

Total People Served

	1998	1999	2000	2001
January	4,238	4,781	6,070	6,622
February	5,010	4,185	5,205	6,359
March	3,997	4,606	6,176	7,049
April	4,269	3,869	5,265	5,686
May	3,908	3,785	5,096	5,533
June	3,690	3,784	4,387	5,587
July	4,706	3,338	3,320	4,286
August	4,706	3,402	3,528	4,514
September	4,330	3,890	4,293	5,019
October	5,047	4,028	5,245	6,092
November	5,081	3,969	5,546	6,353
December	5,494	4,194	5,548	5,563
Total	54,476	47,831	59,679	69,027
Monthly Avg.	4,540	3,986	4,973	5,752

Population of the World's Largest Cities

> **Suggested Activity:** Chose a city and sign the population to a partner, who then identifies the city.

Projected Populations for 2015

Tokyo, Japan	28,887,659
Mexico City, Mexico	19,180,723
Sao Paulo, Brazil	20,320,481
New York City, US	17,602,326
Bombay, India	26,218,015
Shanghai, China	17,969,167
Los Angeles, US	14,218,246
Calcutta, India	17,305,592
Buenos Aires, Argentina	13,856,834
Seoul, South Korea	12,980,908
Beijing, China	15,570,622
Osaka, Japan	10,609,000
Lagos, Nigeria	24,640,010
Rio de Janeiro, Brazil	11,860,751
Delhi, India	16,860,473

The Greatest Show on Earth

> **Suggested Activity:** Using the following circus trivia, ask and answer the questions below with a partner:

1. How many horses does the circus own?
2. How many pounds of carrots are consumed each year?
3. How many countries does the circus go to?
4. How much does the train weigh fully loaded?
5. How many lions, tigers, and bears does the circus have altogether?
6. How many hours does it take to set up for a performance?
7. How many different costumes do they have?
8. How many people see the circus each year?
9. How many performances are given each year?
10. How many loaves of bread do the animals eat in a year?

Circus Trivia

Entertains 25 million people in 97 countries each year
Gives 1,075 performances each year
Uses more than 1,000 costumes
Takes about 8 hours to set up before a performance

Animals:	42 elephants 10 lions 14 tigers 6 bears 33 horses 2 camels 2 llamas 4 zebras	
Each year the animals eat:		364 tons of hay 46,800 pounds of meat 62,400 pounds of carrots 39,000 pounds of apples 15,288 loaves of bread

Circus train: has 53 cars; the fully loaded train weighs 1.5 billion pounds

Telephone Game

> **Suggested Activity:** Divide into equal groups and form lines. The first person in each line faces the instructor, the rest turn around. The instructor signs one of the following numbers including the context prompt one time only to the front row of students. They then turn and tap the next person in line, and sign the same number with context, one time only. The process continues through the line until the last person has seen the number. That person comes to the front of the line and signs it back to the instructor. Teams with the correct number score one point.

October 1998

$1,282

Year 1967

119,259,583,991

7,869 horses

Year 1863

17,712 people

12,823,555,477

May 2001

5,555 elephants

Total 69,027

$33,209

93,849,770

533 cars

August 1999

Year 1776

8,022 lions

27,357,045,839

Total 54,476

Year 1994

Unit Four: Telephone Numbers, Addresses, Zip Codes, and Social Security Numbers

- **Warm-Up Exercises**
- **Overview**
- **Drills: Telephone Numbers**
  Zip Codes
- **Activities: Business Cards**
  How Far?
  Dewey Decimal Game
  Number Relay

Warm-Up Exercises

Shoulder Shrugs: Slowly raise and drop shoulders several times.

The Swan Dive: Slowly stretch arms above your head until they meet, palms together. Gently lower them to shoulder level, palms up. Repeat.

Finger Lifts: Place hand palm down on a table or flat surface and slowly raise and lower each finger. Repeat with the other hand.

Full Arm Stretch: Hold arm out parallel to the floor, palm down. Lock elbow. Raise your hand so the fingertips point to the ceiling. With the other hand, gently press the raised fingers back toward your body for a five-count. Alternate with the other hand. Repeat twice.

Palm Press: Press palms together in front of your body. Keeping your elbows high, use the right palm to gently and slowly push the left palm backwards, from the wrist only, toward the left elbow. Slowly and gently, use the left palm to push the right palm backwards, from the wrist only, toward the right elbow. Repeat several times.

The Frankenstein: With arms stretched out in front of you, palms down, slowly open and close hands, stretching the fingers apart as far as possible. Repeat several times.

Wrist Revolutions: With closed hands, slowly rotate wrists in toward each other several times. Then rotate wrists away from each other several times.

Overview

Telephone Numbers

Telephone numbers can be signed in a variety of ways by incorporating natural groupings or easily remembered number pairings. Note the variations for the telephone number 365-4639 in the following examples:

3-6-5-4-6-3-9	3-6-5-46-39	3-65-46-39

Addresses

Addresses can be also grouped/paired. Note the variations in the following examples:

3-26 Sycamore Dr.	6-8-7-5 Elm Ave.	1-4-2-8-4 Oak St.
3-2-6 Sycamore Dr.	68-75 Elm Ave.	14-2-84 Oak St.
		1-42-84 Oak St.

Zip Codes

Zip codes follow the same patterns:

9-2-4-3-1
9-24-31

Social Security Numbers

Social Security numbers also follow the same patterns:

2-4-0 (pause) 3-4 (pause) 9-7-1-6
2-4-0 (pause) 3-4 (pause) 97-16
2-40-34-97-16

Drill: Telephone Numbers

243-5809	770-4201	333-6644
734-1844	338-7200	562-5485
277-7851	727-8961	353-2001
264-0218	688-3550	258-0581
827-4449	586-6945	463-3005
495-6559	248-7880	235-7743
745-7715	786-1319	533-5191
274-7296	871-6489	750-0750
562-4913	589-3797	722-1909
345-9905	885-4899	907-3456
522-5200	474-7055	542-1207
333-6620	887-1186	495-1447
349-9343	586-1820	694-2254
349-6023	478-1701	586-8164
892-8714	588-5018	321-2271
561-2454	272-4904	566-0777
561-2488	279-1300	625-5268
376-4000	690-4850	522-2217
887-7575	563-0909	955-8770
694-4338	239-1888	352-0135
272-9193	266-9911	435-2445
454-9800	891-1441	333-8102
276-8917	822-3780	265-1710
257-5220	762-0851	791-2759
277-0045	952-2391	245-0126
562-2010	251-0701	688-9897
345-0707	538-8239	533-4487
999-9951	789-2181	587-4169
783-1122	277-2511	522-1379
293-3014	262-9281	698-3612
338-6626	345-8778	463-3005
337-6086	847-0930	903-0762
338-1122	955-7607	274-8523
337-7316	735-2964	651-5744
248-4552	542-8719	782-6090

Drill: Zip Codes

99508	99801	48864
84405	84107	21144
27709	80401	97211
48912	33308	33612
94539	60974	20707

20002	98122	60077
94577	20902	48821
90713	90808	98116
20771	30602	45662
90006	55102	74128

03301	33480	97361
48813	46204	33308
61531	33733	20850
14623	85718	20910
43123	48312	53190

32561	60435	48066
06053	27233	40391
46350	85635	55330
87109	45855	34748
21222	97710	02886

82604	28153	58767
14414	87018	38632
68104	59771	40214
66110	46540	06040
80219	77207	35807

58501	03244	87113
53222	25064	98112
57103	76707	37397
12203	11767	49009
60089	95616	38305

28621	10011	08852
55104	66106	40291
04813	99567	39821
21109	87694	53877
64970	72316	82169

Business Cards

> **Suggested Activity:** Using the following "business cards" practice signing addresses, including zip codes and telephone numbers. (Collect real business cards for additional practice.)

UNIVERSAL CLEANING, INC.
Chester Shonkwiler, Manager
12895 Oneida Woods Trail
Pewamo,VA 59867
(272) 982-5196

Real Estate Associates
Sabrina Polihonki
496 Plum Tree Circle
Silver Springs, MD 20910
[illegible]

Daniel L. Esmay
Attorney at Law
2978 Binghamton Drive
Jacksonville, FL 68253
(321) 641-8152

General Motors, Operations
Marcus A. Swartz
TPC West 660 South Blvd
Raleigh, NC 39521
(364) 249-8573

Statewide Services for the Deaf
Michael Douglas, CI & CT
202 E. Kalamazoo Drive, #200-A
Gaylord, MO 43951
(876) 634-8767
www.mdouglasshi.org

Fine Jewelry
Carl Greve, CEO
317 S. W. Morrison Street
Portland, OR 50279
(800) 284-4420
egreve@carlgreve.com

THE WOODEN SKATE
Olivia Hayden-Meyers, Owner
4524 Wild Blossom Lane
Springfield, IL 36481
(482) 346-7524

Rochelle Jackson, CI & CT
Nationally Certified Interpreter
635 Hubbard Hill Lane
Albany, NY 99957
(663) 524-0122 Voice/TTY

HICKS STUDIO
16927 Sycamore Street
Baltimore, Maryland 21207
(410) 658-2369

FAMILY DENTISTRY
Patricia Jury-Cranson, D.D.S.
3606 Nature Bounty Way
Sheridan, LA 69586
(589) 472-3614

THE MAC
Randall Joseph Emery, Associate
3708 Spike Lane
Hudson, TN 64827
(461) 893-4695

O'BRIEN AGENCY, INC.
Tony O'Brien, Sr., CEO
7200 N. Colby Lake Road
Laingsburg, MA 82591
(225) 347-6914

How Far?

> **Suggested Activity:** With a partner, take turns answering the questions below, incorporating the appropriate ASL signs for cities and states.

1. How far is it between St. Louis and Detroit?
2. How far is it between Atlanta and Washington D.C.?
3. How far is it between Phoenix and Boston?
4. How far is it between New Orleans and San Francisco?
5. How far is it between Buffalo and Los Angeles?
6. How far is it between San Francisco and Atlanta?
7. How far is it between Los Angeles and Phoenix?
8. How far is it between Detroit and New Orleans?
9. How far is it between Boston and Buffalo?
10. How far is it between Washington D.C. and St. Louis?

Distance in miles to/from	**Atlanta, GA**	**Boston, MA**	**Buffalo, NY**	**Detroit, MI**	**Los Angeles, CA**	**New Orleans, LA**	**Phoenix, AZ**	**St. Louis, MO**	**San Francisco, CA**	**Washington, D.C.**
Atlanta, GA	....	933	695	595	1935	427	1592	467	2133	542
Boston, MA	933	....	398	613	2590	1359	2295	1036	2696	392
Buffalo, NY	695	398	....	218	2195	1087	1904	662	2298	290
Detroit, MI	595	613	218	....	1976	938	1685	452	2087	397
Los Angeles, CA	1935	2590	2195	1976	....	1675	357	1585	345	2295
New Orleans, LA	427	1359	1087	938	1675	....	1318	1433	1898	968
Phoenix, AZ	1592	2295	1904	1685	357	1318	....	1270	652	1980
St. Louis, MO	467	1036	662	452	1585	1433	1270	....	1738	710
San Francisco, CA	2133	2696	2298	2087	345	1898	652	1738	....	2437
Washington D.C.	542	392	290	397	2295	968	1980	710	2437	....

Dewey Decimal Game

> **Suggested Activity:** Divide into pairs. Each student takes a different list of Dewey Decimal System numbers for a variety of topics. Ask and answer the following questions using the tables below.

1. Where can I find information about the Electoral College?
2. How about information on parrots?
3. Where are the books on dinosaurs?
4. Where can I find Miss Manners' books?
5. Where would I find Walt Whitman's "Leaves of Grass"?
6. I need a book of Grimms' Fairy Tales.
7. Where can I find a book about volcanoes?
8. How can I find out when the Americans with Disabilities Act was passed?
9. Where can I find pictures of poison ivy?
10. I need information about the moons of Saturn.

Dewey Decimal System

300	SOCIAL SCIENCES, SOCIOLOGY & ANTHROPOLOGY	800	LITERATURE, RHETORIC & CRITICISM
310	Statistics	810	American literature in English
320	Political science	820	English & Old English literatures
330	Economics	830	German & related literatures
340	Law	840	French & related literatures
350	Public administration & military science	850	Italian, Romanian & related literatures
360	Social problems & social services	860	Spanish & Portuguese literatures
370	Education	870	Latin & Italic literatures
380	Commerce, communication & transportation	880	Classical & modern Greek literatures
390	Customs, etiquette & folklore	890	Other literatures

Dewey DecimalSystem—cont'd

500	**SCIENCE**		
510	Mathematics		
520	Astronomy		
530	Physics		
540	Chemistry		
550	Earth sciences & geology		
560	Fossils & prehistoric life		
570	Biology & life sciences		
580	Plants (Botany)		
590	Animals (Zoology)		

Number Relay

> **Suggested Activity:** Divide into teams and form lines. The first person in each line goes to the blackboard, ready to write. The instructor picks a number from the list below and signs it. The first student to correctly write the number on the board wins a point for their team. Students then pass the chalk to the next student in line and go to the back of the line.

Social Security: 379-74-6567
Phone number: 352-4114
4,382,511 people
23 camels
666 tons of hay
12 hours a day
101 Dalmatians
Social Security: 289-11-8549
1,500 daily calories
Social Security: 357-69-3232
42,469 dollars per year
Phone number: 810-876-2141
808 pounds of carrots
$3,327
73 years old
Phone number: 287-9014
$100,000
11 sisters
Social Security number: 068-49-1835
50 states
29 llamas

Unit Five: Time and Age

- **Warm-Up Exercises**
- **Overview**
- **Drill: Time**
- **Activities: Don't Miss the Bus!**
  Numbers Are from Venus and Mars and . . .
  Day Planner
  Planner

Warm-Up Exercises

Shoulder Shrugs: Slowly raise and drop shoulders several times.

The Swan Dive: Slowly stretch arms above your head until they meet, palms together. Gently lower them to shoulder level, palms up. Repeat.

Finger Lifts: Place hand palm down on a table or flat surface and slowly raise and lower each finger. Repeat with the other hand.

Full Arm Stretch: Hold arm out parallel to the floor, palm down. Lock elbow. Raise your hand so the fingertips point to the ceiling. With the other hand, gently press the raised fingers back toward your body for a five-count. Alternate with the other hand. Repeat twice.

Palm Press: Press palms together in front of your body. Keeping your elbows high, use the right palm to gently and slowly push the left palm backwards, from the wrist only, toward the left elbow. Slowly and gently, use the left palm to push the right palm backwards, from the wrist only, toward the right elbow. Repeat several times.

The Frankenstein: With arms stretched out in front of you, palms down, slowly open and close hands, stretching the fingers apart as far as possible. Repeat several times.

Wrist Revolutions: With closed hands, slowly rotate wrists in toward each other several times. Then rotate wrists away from each other several times.

Overview

Time

Time is signed like digital clock time, with TIME incorporated in the message. "A quarter past 10" is signed TIME 10 + 15. "A quarter 'til 11:00" is signed TIME 10 + 45.

When signing "on the hour" (5:00, 3:00, 9:00), the number sign incorporates a small shake, unless the sign already has movement incorporated into it (10, 11, 12).

Two variants are used when signing "on the hour," one where the dominant hand index finger taps the passive wrist and then moves into the number sign, and one where the base of the palm/wrist of the dominant hand, which already incorporates the number sign, taps the passive wrist.

When signing 12 o'clock, the signs NOON or MIDNIGHT are used, or the variants NOON (with the incorporated sign 12) or MIDNIGHT (with the incorporated sign 12).

When signing a combination of hours and minutes (5:20, 3:55, 9:07), the hour sign does not shake.

To indicate am or pm use the sign morning, afternoon, or night before signing the time.

Age

Signing age incorporates the sign OLD, as in OLD 7. Less formally, when indicating the ages 1–9 the OLD sign can be dropped and the number itself slides down from the chin. To indicate someone is seven years old, the sign SEVEN, with the index finger touching the chin, drops from the chin to the natural sign space.

To indicate the span of a decade, the "tens" number sign shakes:

Example: Tim is in his 30's

OLD 3 (shake)

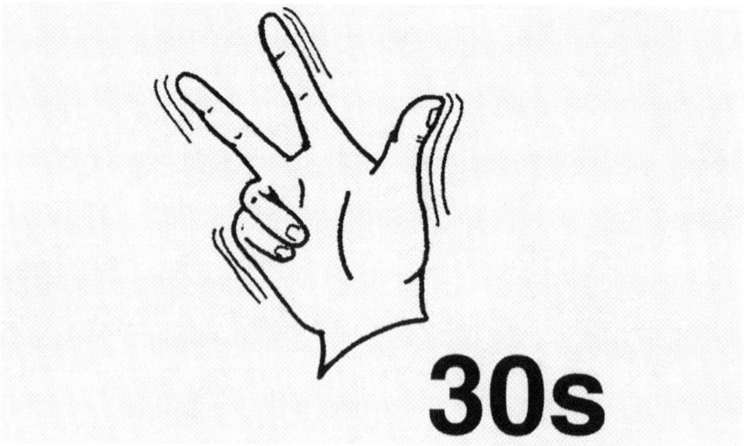

Drill: Time

8:15 am	3:05 am	4:10 am	8:00 am
12:05 pm	10:45 pm	11:15 pm	9:50 pm
6:35 pm	5:55 am	10:35 pm	5:15 am
8:30 pm	1:00 pm	1:05 am	6:00 pm
6:45 am	3:45 am	10:15 pm	11:20 pm
12:15 am	9:10 am	2:25 am	8:50 am
7:15 pm	4:00 pm	8:45 pm	9:00 pm
2:15 am	3:30 pm	4:05 pm	1:10 am
7:00 pm	4:55 am	10:30 am	5:10 am
1:15 pm	12:30 am	2:30 am	8:55 pm
9:30 am	10:25 pm	11:35 pm	3:10 am
9:45 pm	12:50 am	6:25 am	10:40 pm
11:45 pm	5:30 am	5:50 pm	11:40 pm
1:30 am	6:40 pm	7:25 am	12:55 am
12:10 pm	4:50 am	6:30 pm	2:00 am
3:35 am	9:15 am	2:45 pm	11:30 am
4:45 pm	11:25 am	8:10 am	2:20 pm
9:55 pm	3:15 pm	3:40 am	10:00 pm
4:30 pm	6:15 am	10:20 pm	11:00 am
9:05 am	7:20 pm	5:45 am	12:00 am
12:45 pm	8:05 am	5:05 pm	7:40 am
7:30 am	7:45 pm	7:35 pm	3:00 am
5:00 am	4:15 am	6:20 am	1:45 pm
1:25 am	5:40 pm	2:10 am	9:35 pm
1:20 pm	6:50 am	12:40 pm	9:25 am
5:35 am	10:10 pm	11:55 am	2:05 pm
12:20 pm	2:50 am	6:25 pm	11:10 am
9:40 pm	5:25 am	6:05 am	1:35 pm
7:33 am	11:50 pm	9:20 pm	4:25 pm
2:35 pm	10:03 pm	7:50 am	3:20 am
7:05 am	12:25 am	4:35 pm	1:40 pm
3:50 pm	5:20 am	8:25pm	6:10 pm

Suggested Extra Practice: Include practicing the signs for early morning, morning, early afternoon, afternoon, night, and late night with these times.

Don't Miss the Bus!

> **Suggested Activity:** Using the bus schedule provided, answer the questions below with a partner:

1. On Tuesday, the bus leaves the Transit Center at 7:20 am. What time will it arrive at County Hospital?
2. On Saturdays Grant Mall closes at 6:00 pm. If you want to spend at least an hour shopping, what time do you have to catch the bus at 18th & Oak?
3. Your house is a 10-minute walk from 13th & Main and you have an appointment at the County Hospital at 10:45 in the morning. On a weekday, what time do you leave your house to arrive on time for the appointment?
4. On a Saturday, what time would you leave to make the same appointment time?
5. What time do you have to arrive at the Transit Center, if you want to see the 1:30 afternoon movie at the mall on Wednesday? on Saturday?
6. Weekday visiting hours at County Hospital are 8:00 am to 11:15 am and again from 3:00 pm until 8:45 pm. If your apartment is at 13th & Main, what times can you catch a bus and be sure to arrive with time for an hour-and-a-half visit?
7. What time does the last bus get to Grant Mall on a weekday?
8. Approximately what time will you get to 18th & Oak, if you leave the Transit Center at 7:22 pm on a Saturday?
9. What is the earliest time you can take the bus from the Transit Center on a weekday?
10. If I miss the 11:52 am bus from 13th & Main on a Saturday morning, when is the next bus scheduled to leave the same stop?

Bus Schedule

Transit Center	13th & Main	18th & Oak	County Hospital	Grant Mall
Weekdays				
7:20	7:27	7:34	7:43	7:57
9:10	9:17	9:24	9:33	9:43
11:05	11:12	11:19	11:28	11:38
1:00	1:07	1:14	1:23	1:37
3:00	3:08	3:15	3:27	3:40
4:40	4:48	4:55	5:07	5:20
6:15	6:22	6:28	6:37	6:47
8:25	8:32	8:38	8:47	8:57
Saturday				
8:52	8:59	9:04	9:13	9:24
11:45	11:52	11:57	12:06	12:17
2:45	2:52	2:57	3:06	3:17
5:45	5:52	5:57	6:06	6:17
7:22	7:29	7:34	7:43	7:54

Numbers Are from Venus, and Mars and...

> **Suggested Activity:** Using the following statistics, answer the questions below with a partner:

1. Which planet has the largest diameter? What is that diameter?
2. Which planet has the smallest diameter? What is that diameter?
3. How long does it take for Mars to revolve around the sun?
4. How long does it take for Pluto to make one full rotation on its own axis?
5. How far is Neptune from the sun?
6. Which planet takes the most time to revolve around the sun? How long does it take?
7. Which planet takes the least time to revolve around the sun? How long does it take?
8. Which planet is closest to the sun? What is its distance from the sun? How long does it take for it to make one full rotation on its own axis?
9. Cite all the statistics listed here that are related to your favorite planet.
10. What is the period of revolution and the period of rotation for the 3rd planet out from the sun?

Planet	Distance from Sun (miles)	Diameter (miles)	Period of Revolution	Period of Rotation
Mercury	35,960,000	3,100	88 days	57 days
Venus	67,200,000	7,700	225 days	247 days
Earth	92,900,000	7,918	365.25 days	23 hrs. 56 min.
Mars	141,500,000	4,200	687 days	24 hrs. 37 min.
Jupiter	483,400,000	89,000	11.86 years	9 hrs. 55 min.
Saturn	886,200,000	71,500	29.5 years	10 hrs. 14 min.
Uranus	1,783,000,000	30,000	84 years	10 hrs. 45 min.
Neptune	2,790,000,000	27,700	164.75 years	15 hrs. 45min.
Pluto	3,670,000,000	3,664	248.5 years	6.4 days

Day Planner

> **Suggested Activity A:** Divide into pairs. Using the activities below, or your own, fill in the planner on the next page with five activities, in the day and time you will do them. Sign your plans for the week to your partner, who records them on the planner. When finished, compare schedules to make sure theymatch.

> **Suggested Activity B:** In pairs, and using one schedule between you, plan a mutual schedule together, with 10 activities.

Activities

Dinner at Olive Garden
Watch "Wheel of Fortune"
Rollerblading
Pedicure or manicure
Visit grandma
Go to the zoo
ASL class
Study group
Movie
Latte with mother
Water aerobics
Tae Kwan Do class
Couch potato time
Breakfast
Lunch
Dinner
Brunch
Grocery shopping
Laundry
Surfing the Web
Shopping for clothes
Waterskiing

Planner

MONDAY ___/___/___ Activity	TUESDAY ___/___/___ Activity	WEDNESDAY ___/___/___ Activity
7:00 7:15 7:30 7:45	7:00 7:15 7:30 7:45	7:00 7:15 7:30 7:45
8:00 8:15 8:30 8:45	8:00 8:15 8:30 8:45	8:00 8:15 8:30 8:45
9:00 9:15 9:30 9:45	9:00 9:15 9:30 9:45	9:00 9:15 9:30 9:45
10:00 10:15 10:30 10:45	10:00 10:15 10:30 10:45	10:00 10:15 10:30 10:45
11:00 11:15 11:30 11:45	11:00 11:15 11:30 11:45	11:00 11:15 11:30 11:45
12:00 12:15 12:30 12:45	12:00 12:15 12:30 12:45	12:00 12:15 12:30 12:45
1:00 1:15 1:30 1:45	1:00 1:15 1:30 1:45	1:00 1:15 1:30 1:45
2:00 2:15 2:30 2:45	2:00 2:15 2:30 2:45	2:00 2:15 2:30 2:45
3:00 3:15 3:30 3:45	3:00 3:15 3:30 3:45	3:00 3:15 3:30 3:45
4:00 4:15 4:30 4:45	4:00 4:15 4:30 4:45	4:00 4:15 4:30 4:45
5:00 5:15 5:30 5:45	5:00 5:15 5:30 5:45	5:00 5:15 5:30 5:45
6:00 6:15 6:30 6:45	6:00 6:15 6:30 6:45	6:00 6:15 6:30 6:45
7:00 7:15 7:30 7:45	7:00 7:15 7:30 7:45	7:00 7:15 7:30 7:45
8:00 8:15 8:30 8:45	8:00 8:15 8:30 8:45	8:00 8:15 8:30 8:45

Unit Six: Time Measurement

- Warm-Up Exercises
- Overview
- Activities: How Long Does It Take?
  Let's Get Personal
  Getting Creative
  Number Relay

Warm-Up Exercises

Shoulder Shrugs: Slowly raise and drop shoulders several times.

The Swan Dive: Slowly stretch arms above your head until they meet, palms together. Gently lower them to shoulder level, palms up. Repeat.

Finger Lifts: Place hand palm down on a table or flat surface and slowly raise and lower each finger. Repeat with the other hand.

Full Arm Stretch: Hold arm out parallel to the floor, palm down. Lock elbow. Raise your hand so the fingertips point to the ceiling. With the other hand, gently press the raised fingers back toward your body for a five-count. Alternate with the other hand. Repeat twice.

Palm Press: Press palms together in front of your body. Keeping your elbows high, use the right palm to gently and slowly push the left palm backwards, from the wrist only, toward the left elbow. Slowly and gently, use the left palm to push the right palm backwards, from the wrist only, toward the right elbow. Repeat several times.

The Frankenstein: With arms stretched out in front of you, palms down, slowly open and close hands, stretching the fingers apart as far as possible. Repeat several times.

Wrist Revolutions: With closed hands, slowly rotate wrists in toward each other several times. Then rotate wrists away from each other several times.

Overview

Time Measurement

The numbers 1–9 can be incorporated to form a compound sign with MINUTE, HOUR, DAY, WEEK and MONTH.

When incorporating numbers into WEEK (2-WEEK, 8-WEEK), the numbers 1–5 are formed with the knuckles/palm of the dominant hand sliding along the palm of the passive hand. When the numbers 6–9 are incorporated, for visual clarity the sign is raised, so the base of the palm/wrist slides along the upper palm of the passive hand.

When creating tense, there are some variations. For example, when signing PAST-WEEK and FUTURE-WEEK, the numbers 1–3 can be incorporated. However, the sign 4-WEEK-AGO is generally not signed, but converted to PAST-MONTH.

When incorporating numbers into MONTH (3-MONTH, 4-MONTH), the numbers 1–5 are formed with the back of the dominant hand, palm in, sliding down the passive base.

When the numbers 6–9 are incorporated (7-MONTH), this pattern may continue, or a variant may be used. The variant turns palm out, with the base of the palm/wrist sliding down the passive base.

The numbers 1–9 can be incorporated to form a compound sign with YEAR. However, the numbers 1–5 can be incorporated into the sign for NEXT-YEAR and PAST-YEAR.

How Long Does It Take?

> **Suggested Activity:** Create an ASL sentence to share with the rest of the class, about the time it takes for something to happen, based on the information below.

It takes. . .

1. 4 seconds
   to say the McDonald's Big Mac tongue twister: "two all beef patties, special sauce, lettuce, cheese, pickles, onions, on a sesame seed bun."

2. 37 seconds
   to deal a deck of 52 cards.

3. 52 Seconds
   to reach the 86th floor observatory of the Empire State Building by elevator.

4. 1 minute
   for the average adult to read 300 words.

5. 2 minutes, 30 seconds
   to bake a potato in a microwave oven.

6. 3 minutes
   to steep tea.
   to cook a 3-minute egg.

7. 3 minutes, 30 seconds
   to milk a cow producing 10 pounds of milk daily.

8. 12 minutes
   for a bedbug to gorge itself on human blood.

9. 14 minutes
   to broil a 2-inch-thick filet mignon rare.

10. 15 minutes
    for a stripper to lose 36 calories during his or her act.

11. 20 minutes
    to boil lasagna noodles until tender.

12. 36 minutes
    to produce an Oscar Mayer wiener.

13. 48 minutes
    for the average American to commute to work.

How Long Does It Take?—continued

14. 1 hour
    for Parker Brothers to print $392,000 in Monopoly money.
    for a B-58 bomber to travel 1,528 miles.

15. 1 hour 49 minutes
    to view the Hitchcock thriller "Psycho."

16. 1 hour 50 minutes
    for Bobby Fisher to win 19 games of chess in 1970.

17. 3 hours 40 minutes
    to view "Gone With the Wind."

18. 3 hours 59 minutes 51 seconds
    to listen to Marx Brothers radio program excerpts on an album entitled "3 hours, 59 minutes, 51 seconds with the Marx Brothers."

19. 5 hours
    for food to be completely digested in the human stomach.

20. 5 hours 36 minutes
    for a frog embryo to grow 32 cells.

21. 6 hours 15 minutes
    to roast a 22-lb turkey.

22. 10 hours
    for a shearer to clip 200 sheep.

23. 12 hours
    for a caterer's staff of 280 to set tables for a dinner party for 4,000 people.

24. 15 hours
    for a 1- to 3-month-old infant to get his daily sleep requirement

25. 33 hours 29 minutes 30 seconds
    for Charles A. Lindbergh to fly solo from Minneola, New York nonstop to Paris in 1927 in The Spirit of St. Louis.

26. 8 days
    for a pair of average-quality pantyhose to wear out, according to the "Consumers Report Buying Guide."

Let's Get Personal

> **Suggested Activity:** With a partner, share the following numerical information (factual or invented). Be sure to use appropriate ASL structure and grammatical features.

1. Sports Trivia:
   - Number of holes in golf?
   - Length of an Olympic sized pool?
   - Laps on a track to run a mile?
   - Length of a football field?

2. Dream Vacation:
   - Seat number?
   - Hours by plane?
   - Time plane took off? Landed?
   - Length of stay?

3. Home Sweet Home:
   - Total square footage?
   - Size of lot?
   - Size of master bedroom?
   - Number of closets?

Getting Creative

> **Suggested Activity:** With a partner, create a story incorporating the following numeric information.

1. **High School Years:**
   Number of students in each grade
   Number of periods in the school day
   Number of male teachers you had
   Your locker combination

2. **College Life:**
   Years attended
   Total enrollment
   Credit hours taken
   Number of times you changed your major

3. **News Flash:**
   Date
   Time
   Number of rioters
   Hours spent at the hospital

4. **Directions:**
   Highway numbers
   Exit numbers
   House number
   Phone number

5. **Birthday Girl:**
   Date of birthday
   Number of candles
   Number of presents
   Number of people at the party

6. **Public Transportation:**
   Bus number
   Time it takes to get where you are going
   Number of transfers
   Time of day

Number Relay

> **Suggested Activity:** Divide into teams and form lines. The first person in each line goes to the blackboard, ready to write. The instructor signs an item from the list below. The first student to correctly write the number on the board wins a point for his/her team. Students then pass the chalk to the next student in line and go to the back of the line.

$3,314

Year 1952

Phone number: (714) 425-0552

84,123 pineapples

$7,811

Year 1973

Phone number: (410) 269-7697

49,017 buttons

2,566 pencils

Year 1991

Phone number: (302) 284-8599

61,883 tangerines

Student number: 00185

6,728 flags

Year 1825

Phone number: (787) 870-3541

Student number: 34648

5,215 compact discs

$8,063

Year 1969

Phone number: (207) 561-4500

Student number: 55330

Phone number: (616) 927-7174

$5,940

Year 1721

Unit Seven: Decades and Centuries

- Warm-Up Exercises
- Overview
- Drill: Years
- Activities: They Lived, They Died
  100 Freestyle Olympic Champions
  School District Enrollment
  Average SAT Test Scores

Warm-Up Exercises

Shoulder Shrugs: Slowly raise and drop shoulders several times.

The Swan Dive: Slowly stretch arms above your head until they meet, palms together. Gently lower them to shoulder level, palms up. Repeat.

Finger Lifts: Place hand palm down on a table or flat surface and slowly raise and lower each finger. Repeat with the other hand.

Full Arm Stretch: Hold arm out parallel to the floor, palm down. Lock elbow. Raise your hand so the fingertips point to the ceiling. With the other hand, gently press the raised fingers back toward your body for a five-count. Alternate with the other hand. Repeat twice.

Palm Press: Press palms together in front of your body. Keeping your elbows high, use the right palm to gently and slowly push the left palm backwards, from the wrist only, toward the left elbow. Slowly and gently, use the left palm to push the right palm backwards, from the wrist only, toward the right elbow. Repeat several times.

The Frankenstein: With arms stretched out in front of you, palms down, slowly open and close hands, stretching the fingers apart as far as possible. Repeat several times.

Wrist Revolutions: With closed hands, slowly rotate wrists in toward each other several times. Then rotate wrists away from each other several times.

Overview

Decades

As when signing decade-related age information, the span of a decade is signed by shaking the "tens" number sign:

During the 1970s
HAPPEN 197(shake)

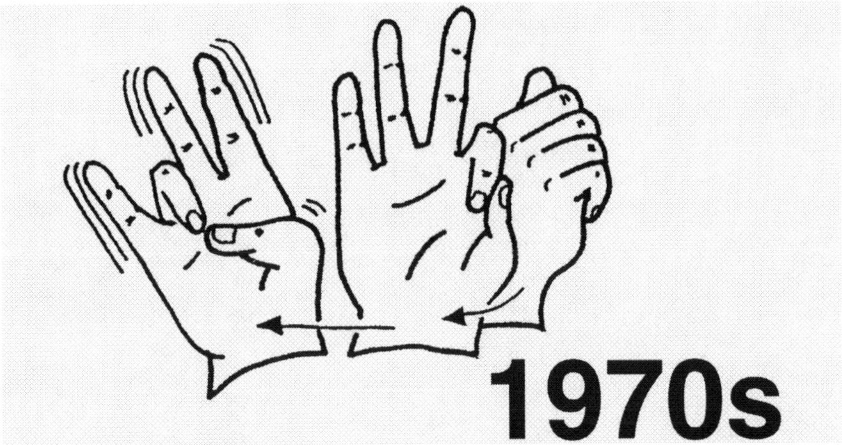

A handshape is sometimes used for "apostrophe S," where the ASL manual alphabet "S" twists from palm out to palm in. This variant would then be 19 70 + 'S (palm out to palm in).

Centuries

A translation occurs when signing a specific century. For example, when discussing the 19th century, it is generally converted to its meaning of "the 1800s," and is signed 18 + C (and the C shakes). However, when talking specifically about the year 1800, sign 18-0-0.

The "apostrophe S," variant is also sometimes used for centuries. "The 1800s" would then be 18 C + 'S (palm out to palm in) or 1800 + 'S.

Drill: Years

1983	1510	1911	1947
1504	1897	1929	1743
1936	1955	1853	1982
1805	1923	1960	1735
1916	1991	1609	1815
1854	1956	1949	1588
1922	1486	1995	1927
1967	1812	1895	1761
1924	1850	1948	1907
1970	1963	1875	1952
1720	1526	1925	1940
1040	1713	2005	1225
1992	1972	2036	1946
1981	1608	1592	1959
1842	1980	1808	1906
1976	1988	1723	1632
2000	1873	1738	1619
1759	1933	1765	1928
1926	1454	1444	1864
1971	1987	1921	2002
1999	1990	1868	1958
1827	1910	1311	1939
1931	1937	1403	1776
1829	1961	2010	1658
1646	1622	1978	1408
1957	1517	1965	1974
1920	1901	1966	1834
1862	1913	1945	1798
1884	1930	1602	1741
1950	1989	1580	1893
1980	1977	1703	1851
1994	1918	1696	1786
1400s	1800s	1700s	1900s
the 17th Century	the 20th Century	the 16th Century	the 7th Century

They Lived, They Died

> **Suggested Activity:** In groups of three, one student fingerspells a name, another signs when that person was born, and a third signs when the person died.

Name	Born	Died
William Shakespeare	1564	1616
Erma Bombeck	1927	1996
Hannibal	247 B.C.	183 B.C.
Mary Shelley	1797	1851
Red Skelton	1913	1997
Edgar Allan Poe	1809	1849
Martin Luther King, Jr.	1929	1968
Kurt Cobain	1967	1994
Tilly Edinger	1897	1967
Indira Gandhi	1917	1984
Akira Kurosawa	1910	1998
Henry VIII	1491	1547
Florence Griffith Joyner	1959	1998
Davy Crockett	1786	1836
Princess Diana	1961	1997
Julius Caesar	100 B.C.	44 B.C.
Lou Fant	1932	2001
Isadora Duncan	1878	1927
Orville Redenbacher	1907	1995
John Milton	1608	1674
James Herriot	1916	1995
Beatrix Potter	1866	1943
Dante	1265	1321
Richard Farnsworth	1920	2000
Geronimo	1829	1909
Gianlorenzo Bernini	1598	1680
Tupac Shakur	1971	1996
Joan of Arc	1414	1431
Joe DiMaggio	1914	1999
Louis Armstrong	1900	1971
Jim Henson	1936	1990
Lydia Liliuokalani	1838	1917
Marie Phillip	1953	1997
Malcolm X	1925	1965
Juliette Gordon Low	1860	1927
Gene Rodenberry	1921	1991
Charles Schulz	1922	2000
Deng Xiaopeng	1904	1997
Margaret Hamilton	1902	1985
Vincent Price	1911	1993
Laura Redden Searing	1840	1923

100 Freestyle Olympic Champions

> **Suggested Activity:** In groups of three, one student signs a year, the next student spells the name of the swimmer, and the third student signs the corresponding Olympic time.

Year	Swimmer	Olympic Time (minutes/seconds)
1896	Alfred Hajos, Hungary	1:22.20
1904	Zolton de Halmay, Hungary	1:02.80
1908	Charles Daniel, US	1:05.60
1912	Duke Kahanmoku, US	1:03.40
1920	Duke Kahanmoku, US	1:01.40
1924	Johnny Weismuller, US	59.00
1928	Johnny Weismuller, US	58.60
1932	Yasuji Miyazaki, Japan	58.20
1936	Ferenc Csik, Hungary	57.60
1948	Wally Ris, US	57.30
1952	Clark Scholes, US	57.40
1956	Jon Henricks, Australia	55.40
1960	John Devitt, Australia	55.20
1964	Don Schollander, US	53.40
1968	Mike Wenden, Australia	52.20
1972	Mark Spitz, US	51.20
1976	Jim Montgomery, US	49.99
1980	Jog Worthe, E. Germany	50.40
1984	Rowdy Gaines, US	49.80
1988	Matt Biondi, US	48.63
1992	Aleksandr Popov, Unified team	49.02
1996	Aleksandr Popov, Russia	48.74
2000	Peter Vanden Hoogenband, Denmark	47.84

School District Enrollment

> **Suggested Activity:** With a partner, take turns asking and answering the following questions using the chart provided:

1. How many elementary students were enrolled in 1995?
2. How many secondary students were enrolled in 1987?
3. How many students were receiving special services in 2000?
4. What was the total number of students enrolled in 1981?
5. How many students were receiving special services in 1989?
6. How many elementary students were enrolled in 1998?
7. How many secondary students were enrolled in 1983?
8. What was the total number of students enrolled in 1990?
9. How many students were receiving special services in 1986?
10. How many elementary students were enrolled in 1980?

School District Enrollment, 1980–2000

Year	No. of Elementary Students	No. of Secondary Students	No. of Special Services Students	Total No. of Students
1980	21,763	15,398	187	37,348
1981	22,433	16,402	237	39,072
1982	22,450	17,151	238	39,839
1983	21,510	17,341	322	39,173
1984	21,232	17,800	373	39,405
1985	21,634	18,093	414	40,141
1986	21,461	18,250	431	39,606
1987	21,283	17,887	436	39,606
1988	21,058	17,429	409	38,896
1989	20,596	16,360	376	36,908
1990	20,232	16,190	396	36,737
1991	20,596	17,378	361	37,357
1992	21,472	17,378	441	39,291
1993	21,971	17,832	624	40,427
1994	23,092	18,341	630	42,063
1995	23,440	18,237	749	42,426
1996	23,834	17,609	554	41,997
1997	23,511	16,890	506	40,907
1998	23,618	16,117	585	40,320
1999	23,943	16,311	565	40,819
2000	25,046	16,665	511	42,222

Average SAT Test Scores

> **Suggested Activity:** Using the statistics provided, answer the questions below with a partner. Use appropriate ASL signs or fingerspelling for the states.

1. What were the 1980 and 1990 verbal scores for Indiana?
2. When Delaware's verbal score was 431, what was its math score?
3. What year did New Jersey students score 418 in the verbal portion?
4. What was the 1980 total for Vermont?
5. When students in Hawaii scored 481 in the math portion, what was their score in the verbal portion?
6. The year Florida had a total score of 888, what was Oregon's total score?
7. For the students in Texas, which score was higher: the 1990 total or the 1980 math?
8. What year did Maine score 463 in the math portion?
9. When Rhode Island scored 422 in the verbal portion, what was Vermont's math score?
10. When California's total was 903, what was Virginia's total?

Statewide SAT Scores

	1980			1990		
State	**Verbal**	**Math**	**Total**	**Verbal**	**Math**	**Total**
California	424	472	896	419	484	903
Delaware	431	469	900	433	470	903
Florida	424	464	888	418	466	884
Georgia	389	425	814	401	443	844
Hawaii	396	472	868	404	481	885
Indiana	407	450	857	408	459	867
Maine	427	467	894	423	463	886
Maryland	422	463	885	430	478	908
New Jersey	415	452	867	418	473	891
Oregon	427	465	892	439	484	923
Rhode Island	417	458	875	422	461	883
Texas	416	455	871	413	461	874
Vermont	432	468	900	431	466	897
Virginia	423	460	883	425	470	895

Unit Eight: Money and Percents

- **Warm-Up Exercises**
- **Overview**
- **Activities:** Here's a Tip
  Home Prices in the USA
  Let's Buy a House
  Meal-Lodging Cost Index
  Getting Creative
  Let's Make a Car Deal
  Vegetarian Restaurant
  Shopping Trends
  Do the Math

Warm-Up Exercises

Shoulder Shrugs: Slowly raise and drop shoulders several times.

The Swan Dive: Slowly stretch arms above your head until they meet, palms together. Gently lower them to shoulder level, palms up. Repeat.

Finger Lifts: Place hand palm down on a table or flat surface and slowly raise and lower each finger. Repeat with the other hand.

Full Arm Stretch: Hold arm out parallel to the floor, palm down. Lock elbow. Raise your hand so the fingertips point to the ceiling. With the other hand, gently press the raised fingers back toward your body for a five-count. Alternate with the other hand. Repeat twice.

Palm Press: Press palms together in front of your body. Keeping your elbows high, use the right palm to gently and slowly push the left palm backwards, from the wrist only, toward the left elbow. Slowly and gently, use the left palm to push the right palm backwards, from the wrist only, toward the right elbow. Repeat several times.

The Frankenstein: With arms stretched out in front of you, palms down, slowly open and close hands, stretching the fingers apart as far as possible. Repeat several times.

Wrist Revolutions: With closed hands, slowly rotate wrists in toward each other several times. Then rotate wrists away from each other several times.

Overview

Money

When signing dollar amounts, sign the number, then sign DOLLAR. A standard variant is used for 1–9 dollars, which twists the number sign from palm out to palm in. However, when signing 10 dollars and up, sign the number, then sign DOLLAR.

"Cents" values are signed by touching the forehead with the index finger (palm in). CENT may be signed before or after the number (e.g., a "quarter" can be signed as either CENT 25 or 25 CENT).

When signing 1–9 dollars with cents, as in $4.75, twist the 4 palm-out to palm-in, then return to palm-out for the 75 cents. "Cents" is implied, and is thus not signed.

There are a number of approaches used when signing dollar and cent combinations above 9 dollars. For example, $63.28 may be signed:

63 DOLLAR 28CENT

63 DOLLAR 28

The decimal point in ASL is signed using the handshape of a boxed X, and is included in the following approach:

DOLLAR 63 DECIMAL-POINT 28

Percents

Percents are signed as follows: the number is signed, palm out, followed by sign for PERCENT.

Here's a Tip

> **Suggested Activity:** Choose a dollar amount. In pairs, one person calculates the total bill with a 15% tip, and one with a 20 % tip. For example, a check amount of $18.00 with a 15% tip is $20.70, and $21.60 with a 20% tip. ($18.00 + $2.70; $18.00 + $3.60)

Check Amount	15%	20%
$1.00	$0.15	$0.20
$3.00	$0.45	$0.60
$5.00	$0.75	$1.00
$7.00	$1.05	$1.40
$9.00	$1.35	$1.80
$11.00	$1.65	$2.20
$12.00	$1.80	$2.40
$13.00	$1.95	$2.60
$14.00	$2.10	$2.80
$15.00	$2.25	$3.00
$16.00	$2.40	$3.20
$17.00	$2.55	$3.40
$18.00	$2.70	$3.60
$19.00	$2.85	$3.80
$20.00	$3.00	$4.00
$21.00	$3.15	$4.20
$22.00	$3.30	$4.40
$23.00	$3.45	$4.60
$24.00	$3.60	$4.80
$25.00	$3.75	$5.00
$26.00	$3.90	$5.20
$27.00	$4.05	$5.40
$28.00	$4.20	$5.60
$29.00	$4.35	$5.80
$30.00	$4.50	$6.00
$37.00	$5.55	$7.40
$42.00	$6.30	$8.40
$49.00	$7.35	$9.80
$55.00	$8.25	$11.00
$61.00	$9.15	$12.20
$63.00	$9.45	$12.60
$69.00	$10.35	$13.80
$70.00	$10.50	$14.00
$74.00	$11.10	$14.80
$82.00	$12.30	$16.40
$86.00	$12.90	$17.20
$90.00	$13.50	$18.00
$95.00	$14.25	$19.00
$100.00	$15.00	$20.00

Home Prices in the USA

> **Suggested Activity:** With a partner, one person signs/fingerspells a location, and the other responds with the corresponding price of a home there. Use the appropriate ASL sign or fingerspelling for the states.

1999 Home Prices for US Cities

Home = 2,200 square feet, 4-bedrooms, $2^1/_2$ baths, family room, and double-car garage. Located in an area desirable for mid-level executive.

City	Price	City	Price
Montgomery, AL	$107,215	Omaha, NE	$108,635
Juneau, AK	$133,330	Reno, NV	$131,444
Tucson, AZ	$128,533	Nashua, NH	$210,777
Little Rock, AR	$109,750	Hunterdon, NJ	$243,250
Beverly Hills, CA	$916,667	Albuquerque, NM	$140,750
Denver, CO	$108,167	Rochester, NY	$150,000
Danbury, CT	$257,665	Raleigh, NC	$177,300
Dover, DE	$128,500	Fargo, ND	$153,400
Tallahassee, FL	$124,000	Toledo, OH	$124,000
Savannah, GA	$107,750	Tulsa, OK	$116,800
Honolulu, HI	$438,333	Portland, OR	$116,296
Boise, ID	$82,677	Harrisburg, PA	$158,881
Bloomington, IL	$114,634	Providence, RI	$223,669
South Bend, IN	$91,600	Charleston, SC	$128,150
Des Moines, IA	$126,688	Rapid City, SD	$118,025
Topeka, KS	$130,583	Nashville, TN	$129,188
Louisville, KY	$123,667	Arlington, TX	$98,332
Shreveport, LA	$121,225	Salt Lake City, UT	$125,500
Bangor, ME	$167,230	Burlington, VT	$218,143 Baltimore,
MD	$189,333	Richmond, VA	$124,844 Worchester, MA
$206,867	Seattle, WA		$180,833 East Lansing, MI
$147,783	Charleston, WV		$131,667 St. Paul, MN
$143,466	Milwaukee, WI		$170,900 Jackson, MS
$102,470	Cheyenne, WY		$110,000 Kansas City, MO
$119,975	Vancouver, Canada		$288,257 Great Falls, MT $125,833

Let's Buy a House

> **Suggested Activity:** One partner is a real estate agent who is trying to match a potential buyer with the right home from the listings below. Ask questions about the buyer's requirements for a house using input from the ads below, and select three ads that might meet them.

Home Listings

Almost 1 Acre!
4 BR, 2.5 BA, double garage
$248,000

Up On Top
Great Views of the mountains!
2,296 SqFt PLUS
16,542 SqFt lot and horse property
$197,000

Assumable Mortgage
3 BR, 2.5 BA
Close to schools
$158,900

Fixer Upper Duplex
Ranch Style 1 BR, 1 BA
4-star energy rating
$89,000

Neptune Lake Condo
2 BR, 1 BA, storage
$59,000

LOG HOME!
16" Alaska Spruce Logs
3–4 BR, modeled after a lodge
built in the 1920's! Features 3 river-rock fireplaces.
$785,000

Hidden Hills Exclusive
3 BR, 2.5 BA, 3-car garage
7,000 SqFt backs up to 10-acre greenbelt. Built in '93
$299,000

Must Sell Now!
3 BR, 2.5 BA, 2,264 SqFt
2 decks, Jacuzzi
$214,000

Great Starter
2 BR, 1.5 BA townhouse
Perfect for first time buyer
$120,000

VA Approved Townhouse
2 BR, 3 BA, carport, small courtyard
Association Dues $210/month

Midtown Construction
5 minutes from downtown!
2,900 SqFt homes on wooded lots
Open house Sunday 1–4

Possible B & B
8 BR, 4 BA
9' ceilings, 3-car garage
4,803 SqFt, built in 1998
$449,900

Move in Now!
3 BR, 2 BA, next to park
Seller pays $2,000 in closing costs!
$156,175

Single Family Homes 1,609–2,400 SqFt
4 Floor plans to choose from!
$187,000–$214,5000

Meal-Lodging Cost Index

> **Suggested Activity:** With a partner, and using the information in the table below, take turns asking and answering the following questions. Use appropriate ASL signs or fingerspelling for the states.

1. What is the range of rates for a single bed in Honolulu, HI?
2. Compare the low and high price for a room at the single corporate rate in Washington, DC.
3. Which city has the most expensive single bed rate?
4. Which city has the cheapest single bed rate?
5. For the 2 cities that have the lowest corporate rate, compare their high corporate rates.
6. If your company allows you to spend $41.00 a day for meals, where can you do business without having to spend extra on food?
7. Compare the low and high single corporate rates in Anchorage with those in San Francisco.
8. If you have $100 a day to spend for meals and lodging combined, which city would you go to and which type of lodging would you choose?
9. Compare the single low and high rates to the double low and high rates for Chicago.
10. Among those cities listed, which would you choose for a vacation? What type of lodging would you choose? Estimate your total expenses for meals and lodging for three days.

Meals and Lodging Costs in Major U.S. Cities
Peak Season 1999

City, State	Single Low	Single High	Single Corporate Low	Single Corporate High	Double Low	Double High	3-Meal Total
Anchorage, AK	$100	$148	$80	$106	$108	$162	$36
Atlanta, GA	$95	$146	$88	$137	$106	$166	$40
Boston, MA	$127	$175	$110	$156	$142	$195	$43
Chicago, IL	$134	$182	$120	$163	$154	$202	$43
Dallas, TX	$80	$127	$73	$114	$93	$156	$36
Honolulu, HI	$139	$202	$119	$178	$141	$202	$45
Las Vegas, NV	$63	$96	$54	$85	$63	$97	$44
Manhattan, NY	$180	$239	$167	$223	$197	$268	$68
New Orleans, LA	$66	$111	$54	$88	$69	$117	$37
Philadelphia, PA	$98	$144	$84	$125	$107	$160	$39
San Francisco, CA	$116	$160	$102	$142	$131	$177	$43
Washington, D.C.	$138	$185	$116	$161	$156	$211	$46

Getting Creative

> **Suggested Activity:** With a partner, create a story incorporating the following numeric information for each topic. Be prepared to share one of your stories in front of your class.

1. Vacation:
    - Date of trip
    - Amount spent on souvenirs
    - Number of suitcases
    - Total cost of trip

2. Grocery Shopping:
    - Store hours
    - Number of registers open
    - Total spent
    - Shopping time

3. Real Estate:
    - Number of bedrooms
    - Number of bathrooms
    - Asking price
    - Purchasing price

4. Personal Ad:
    - Height
    - Weight range
    - Age range
    - Years of education

5. Lottery:
    - Winning numbers
    - Amount before taxes
    - Amount after taxes
    - Number of tickets purchased per year

Let's Make a Car Deal

> **Suggested Activity:** Each student in the class is assigned one of the ads below. One student starts by "calling" one of the phone numbers and arranging to look at the car. The "seller" meets with the "buyer" and tries to sell his or her vehicle.

Classified Ads—Cars and Trucks for Sale

'83 Ford Ranger XL 5 speed $1,950 694-4338	'91 Toyota Landcruiser 117,000 miles $14,700 239-1888
'95 Grand Cherokee V6, 88,000 miles $6,400 522-2379	'85 BMW 2 dr., 2 sets of tires $2,700 387-8734
'91 Jeep 4x4 1.0L, 4 dr, 98,000 miles $5,700 783-7722	'88 Chevy Cavalier 4 dr, tags 11/02 $1,500 564-9193
'98 GMC SLE ½ ton extension cab 30 K miles, $22,600 277-2511	'69 VW Beetle 2K+ miles $450 698-3612
'01 Suburban 1500 36 K mi, 9" tv /vcr $32,750 892-8714	'70 Ford Mustang Hatchback 1 owner $1,800 Firm 522-2217
'80 Toyota Tercel 2 dr., 5 speed, 35 mpg $395 248-7880	'92 Geo Prism 5 speed, 75K miles $3,750 321-2271
2000 Z-71 Extended cab 3rd door, 5.3 L $24,500 obo 786-1319	'55 Chevy ½ ton Stepside $11,000 495-1300
'94 Nissan Sentra Was asking $4,200 NOW $3,350 891-1441	'99 Jeep Wrangler Sport 6 cyl., 34K miles $14,500 566-0777

Vegetarian Restaurant

> **Suggested Activity:** Divide into groups of three. Two students act as restaurant patrons, the third as their server. The patrons order from the menu below. The server writes down the ordered items, and then must calculate the final bill for the patrons. The patrons then calculate their total, including a tip.

MENU

APPETIZERS		
	Fresh Hand Rolled Tamales	$5.99
	Guacamole	$4.99
	Nachos Grande	$6.99
	Chile Con Questa	$3.99
COMBOS		
	Veggie Burrito	$8.99
	Veggie Tacos	$7.99
	Veggie Enchilada	$9.99
	Veggie Chimichanga	$10.99
	Veggie Tamale	$6.99
	Veggie Flauta	$5.99
SIDES		
	Flour Tortillas	$1.75
	Salsa	$2.99
	Guacamole	$4.25
	Sweet Corn Tomalito	$2.50
	Mexican Rice	$1.50
	Black Beans	$2.75
	Chips and Salsa	$3.99
BEVERAGES		
	Herbal Tea	$2.00
	Fruit Juice	$1.75
	Natural Tea	$1.50
	Perrier	$1.25
	Milk	$1.10

Shopping Trends

> **Suggested Activity:** Using the information in the survey below, partners take turns answering the questions below:

1. What percentage of those surveyed shopped at Nordstrom in 2000?
2. What percentage shopped at Fred Meyer in 1996?
3. What percentage shopped at Pricesavers in 1999?
4. What percentage shopped at Costco in 1997?
5. What percentage shopped at Longs in 1998?
6. What percentage shopped at Pay 'N Pak in 1999?
7. What percentage shopped at Sears in 2000?
8. What percentage shopped at Lamonts in 1997?
9. What percentage shopped at JC Penney in 1999?
10. What percentage shopped at Pay 'N Save in 1996?

Shopping Survey Results

(Participant responses to the survey question: Which of these stores have you shopped at in the past 30 days, whether or not you bought anything?)

Store	1996	1997	1998	1999	2000
Costco	35%	36%	34%	32%	42%
Fred Meyer	60%	61%	67%	66%	71%
JC Penney	36%	32%	38%	31%	35%
Lamonts	45%	46%	50%	45%	47%
Longs	42%	37%	30%	34%	33%
Nordstrom	37%	40%	32%	39%	31%
Pay 'N Save	80%	73%	72%	71%	68%
Pay 'N Pak	29%	25%	26%	20%	21%
Pricesavers	28%	31%	44%	45%	51%
Sears	60%	52%	56%	48%	48%

Do the Math

> **Suggested Activity A:** The instructor signs the following math problems without the answer. Students respond with the correct answer.

> **Suggested Activity B:** The instructor writes the following problems on index/flash cards, and distributes them to students. In pairs, they must sign their problem to their partner, who must write the problem down in the form in which it was signed and compute the answer, and sign the answer back to their partner.

10 X 10 = 100	15 -s- 5 = 3	42 – 9 = 31
53 + 14 = 67	300 + 800 = 1,100	62 + 72 = 134
100 – 75 = 25	59 + 95 = 154	5 X 5 = 25
396 X 2 = 792	11 -s- 11 = 1	298 – 98 = 200
78 + 3 = 81	604 – 24 = 580	70 + 80 = 150
13 + 23 = 36	23 + 76 = 99	53 – 33 = 20
19 – 6 = 13	50 -s- 2 = 25	26,015 X 0 = 0
12 X 12 = 144	9,876 – 876 = 9,000	(7 X 7) – 4 = 45
99 -s- 9 = 11	246 + 357 = 603	1 + 2 + 3 + 4 + 5 = 15
178 + 3 = 181	650 + 640 = 1,290	1 X 2 X 3 X 4 X 5 = 120

Unit Nine: Pronouns, Height, and Measurement

- **Warm-Up Exercises**
- **Overview**
- **Activities:** **All about Animals**
  Big and Small
  Let's Get Personal
  Hot, Cold, Rain, Snow
  Favorite Recipes
  Calorie and Fat Content
  Women's Basketball

Warm-Up Exercises

Shoulder Shrugs: Slowly raise and drop shoulders several times.

The Swan Dive: Slowly stretch arms above your head until they meet, palms together. Gently lower them to shoulder level, palms up. Repeat.

Finger Lifts: Place hand palm down on a table or flat surface and slowly raise and lower each finger. Repeat with the other hand.

Full Arm Stretch: Hold arm out parallel to the floor, palm down. Lock elbow. Raise your hand so the fingertips point to the ceiling. With the other hand, gently press the raised fingers back toward your body for a five-count. Alternate with the other hand. Repeat twice.

Palm Press: Press palms together in front of your body. Keeping your elbows high, use the right palm to gently and slowly push the left palm backwards, from the wrist only, toward the left elbow. Slowly and gently, use the left palm to push the right palm backwards, from the wrist only, toward the right elbow. Repeat several times.

The Frankenstein: With arms stretched out in front of you, palms down, slowly open and close hands, stretching the fingers apart as far as possible. Repeat several times.

Wrist Revolutions: With closed hands, slowly rotate wrists in toward each other several times. Then rotate wrists away from each other several times.

Overview

Pronouns

Pronoun incorporation uses both palm orientation and movement to indicate which people are being discussed.

The signs for 2-OF-US, 2-OF-YOU, and 2-OF-THEM use a slight back-and-forth shake between the identified parties. For 2-OF-US, the palm faces in, close to the shoulder, while for 2-OF-YOU and 2-OF-THEM, the palm faces up, shaking between referents.

In the incorporations 3-OF-US, 4-OF-US, etc., the palm orientation is also up, but the movement is a tight counter-clockwise circle for right-handed signers. Left-handed signers make a tight clockwise circle.

Height

Height is described in feet and inches. To sign this, start with the "feet" measurement number, palm in, by the head. Then move the hand out, away from the head, while signing the "inches" measurement number. This context eliminates the need to add signs for feet and inches.

When the person being described is taller than the signer, the signer makes a slight upward movement for the "inches," also palm in. When the person is shorter, the signer makes a slight downward movement, palm in. When the person is approximately the same height, the movement is side-to-side, palm in.

Measurement

Units of measurement are often fingerspelled abbreviations (ft, mm, tsp, lb, oz, mph). "Inches" is typically fingerspelled in contexts other than height, or represented by the sign MEASURE. "Degrees" can be fingerspelled, or represented by the sign TEMPERATURE.

Context is important when applying units of measurement: when talking about a pound of butter, "lb" is appropriate; when talking about a newborn 7-pound 3-ounce baby, the sign WEIGH is used: 7 POUND 3 O-Z.

All about Animals

> **Suggested Activity:** With a partner, pick an animal and sign animal facts back and forth.

Animal Facts

Name	Height/Length	Weight	Other Facts
Grey Wolf	25–32 inches (at shoulder)	175 lbs.	A wolf's howl can be heard as far as 6 miles away. There are 4–7 cubs in a typical litter.
Giraffe	18 feet	1,800 lbs.	A newborn giraffe can be 6 feet tall and weigh 100 pounds. A giraffe's tongue is up to 18 inches long.
African Lion	9 feet	550 lbs.	A pride of lions generally has 20–40 members. Lions can run up to 37 mph for short distances.
Skunk	30 inches	6.5 lbs.	Skunks can squirt their musk up to 12 feet. The smell can be detected as far away as a mile and a half.
African Elephant	10–11.5 feet	6 tons (male) 4 tons (female)	The largest tusk ever recorded was 10 feet long and weighed nearly 230 pounds.
Red Fox	24–42 inches	10–15 lbs.	Foxes dig tunnels that can be up to 30 feet long, leading to a chamber 3–10 feet below ground. There can be as many as 19 entrances to the tunnel.
Black Bear	3 ft (at shoulder) 5–6 feet long	250–600 lbs.	Diet is 75% vegetable matter (berries, nuts, roots).
Moose	6–8 feet	1,300–1,500 lbs.	Moose have a 250-day gestation period. A rack of antlers can span 6 feet.
White Rhino	6.3 feet (height) 12–17 feet (length)	5,000–7,900 lbs.	White rhinos have two horns on their snouts. Only about 17 are known to exist in the wild, and there are about a dozen in captivity.

Big and Small

> **Suggested Activity:** In groups of three, one student fingerspells a category, the second student fingerspells the name of the record holder, and the third the corresponding famous fact.

World Record Holders

Category	Record Holder	Famous Fact
Tallest Tribe	The Watussi of Rowanda, Central Africa	Average 6 ft.
Smallest Tribe	The Mbutsi Pygmies of the Congo	Men: 4 ft. 4 in. Women: 4ft. 1in.
Tallest People	Robert Wadlow, US (male)	8ft. 11 1/10 in.
	Sandy Allen, US (female)	7ft. 7 1/4 in.
Shortest People	John and Greg Rice US (twins) (male)	2 ft. 10 in.
	Paulene Masters, Netherlands (female)	1 ft. 9 3/4 in.
Heaviest People	John Minnoch, US	1,403 lbs.
	Rosalie Bradford, US	1, 202.24 lbs.
Lightest Person	Lucia Xarate, Mexico	26 1/2 in. tall; 13 lbs.
Smallest Waist	Ethel Granger, England	13 in.
Largest Waist	Walter Hudson, US	9 ft. 11 in.
Heaviest Single Birth	Anna Bates, Canada	23 lbs. 12 oz
Biggest Feet	Matthew McGrory, US	28 1/2 size shoes
Biggest Gallbladder	69 year old woman, US	23 lbs.
Heaviest Brain	Brenda Cartwright, US	5 lbs. 1 1/10 oz.
Lightest Brain	Daniel Lyon, Ireland	1 lb. 8 oz.
Longest Hair	Hu Saelo, Thailand	16 ft. 10 in.
Heaviest Breasts	Eve Lolo, France	6 lbs. 2 oz.

Let's Get Personal

> **Suggested Activity:** Go around the room and ask each of your classmates what his/her height is. Record the heights and names. Sort from shortest to tallest.

Example:

4'10"	LeeAnn Smith
5'5"	LaWanda Trubot, Jacob Ivanof, Therese Quendere
6'1"	Marisa Vander Veen, Tyrone Winston

Height feet/inches	**Classmate Names**
________	____
________	____
________	____
________	____
________	____
________	____
________	____
________	____
________	____
________	____
________	____
________	____
________	____
________	____
________	____

Hot, Cold, Rain, Snow

> **Suggested Activity:** With a partner, ask and answer the questions about the weather in the cities listed below.

1. How much snow does Anchorage get in an average year?
2. What is the mean annual temperature for Fairbanks?
3. How much does it generally rain in Seattle in any given year?
4. How much can it rain in Chicago in any given year?
5. How much does it generally snow in Boston in any given year?
6. In an average year, how much snow does New York get?
7. What is the mean annual temperature for Minneapolis?
8. What is the mean annual temperature for San Francisco?
9. What is the average annual rainfall in Denver?
10. What is the average annual snowfall in Washington D.C.?

Weather Statistics

City	Mean Annual Temperature	Average Annual Rain	Average Annual Snow
Anchorage	35	15.2"	69.3"
Boston	51	42.5"	43.1"
Chicago	49	31.7"	39.3"
Denver	50	15.5"	59.0"
Fairbanks	26	11.2"	68.3"
Juneau	40	54.7"	106.4"
Minneapolis	44	25.9"	46.3"
New York	55	40.2"	29.3"
San Francisco	57	20.7"	Trace
Seattle	53	35.6"	14.3"
Washington, D.C.	57	38.9"	16.6"

Favorite Recipes

> **Suggested Activity:** In pairs, one student signs a recipe while the other writes it down. When finished, compare with the original to see if they match. Change roles and repeat, with a different recipe.

GRILLED RATTLESNAKE CHINESE STYLE

1 fresh rattlesnake
1/8 cup soy sauce
1/8 cup fresh lime juice
2 tbsp. sweet sherry

Combine the soy sauce, lime juice, and sherry. Cut snake into pieces. Add the snake and marinate for two hours. Prepare a fire in a charcoal grill. Remove the snake from the marinade and keep the marinade. Thread the snake onto bamboo skewers and grill, basting frequently with the marinade until tender.

APRICOT LOVE POTION

Combine:
1 cup of apricot nectar
1/2 cup of seltzer water
1 tablespoon of honey
1/2 teaspoon of vanilla

Drink while still fizzing. Share with someone you like and see what happens!

PLAY DOUGH (Non-hardening variety)

Mix together:
250 ml flour
125 ml salt
10 ml cream of tartar
250 ml water
Few drops of food coloring

In a pan, heat 2 tbsp (10 ml) vegetable oil. Add the mixed ingredients, and cook 3 minutes. Stir constantly. Let the dough cool. Store in plastic wrap in the refrigerator.

Favorite Recipes—continued

CHOCOLATE CHIRPLE CHIP COOKIES

$2\frac{1}{2}$ cup flour
1 tsp baking soda
1 tsp salt
1 cup butter, softened
$\frac{1}{2}$ cup sugar
$\frac{1}{2}$ cup brown sugar
1 tsp vanilla
2 eggs
10 dry-roasted crickets
1 12-ounce bag chocolate chips
1 cup chopped nuts

Preheat oven to 375. In small bowl, combine flour, baking soda, and salt; set aside. In large bowl, combine butter, sugar, brown sugar and vanilla; beat until creamy. Beat in eggs. Gradually add flour mixture and insects, mix well. Stir in chocolate chips and nuts. Drop by rounded measuring teaspoonfuls onto greased cookie sheet. Bake for 8–10 minutes.

SPICY APPLESAUCE ORNAMENTS (Cinnamon Applesauce Hearts)

1 lb. jar sweetened applesauce
8 oz. cinnamon

Drain jar of applesauce overnight (you will be amazed at how much liquid seeps out). Add cinnamon and mix well. Pat into a ball, pressing hard to solidify and mix. Pat out in 1-cup units onto wax paper. Push to $\frac{1}{2}$" thickness and cut with cookie cutters. . Poke a hole in the top with toothpick. Dry by letting them sit in a warm place for several days, turning them over regularly. When completely dry, hang a ribbon through the hole. Use as a decoration or a sachet. These are NOT edible.

Calorie and Fat Content

> **Suggested Activity:** With a partner, take turns identifying specific candy bars with their calories and fat content by asking and answering the questions below:

1. How many fat grams are in a roll of Life Savers?
2. How many calories are in a Mr. Goodbar?
3. How many fat grams are in a York Peppermint Patty?
4. How many calories are in an Almond Joy?
5. How many fat grams are in box of Junior Mints?
6. How many calories are in a Sugar Daddy?
7. How many fat grams are in box of Good & Plenty?
8. How many calories are in a Kit Kat?
9. How many fat grams are in a Tootsie Roll?
10. How many calories are in a bag of Peanut M & Ms?

Calories and Fat in Candy Bars

Candy Bar	Calories	Fat grams
Almond Joy (1.76 oz)	250	14
Good & Plenty (1.8 oz)	191	0
Hershey's Milk Chocolate (1.55 oz)	240	14
Junior Mints (1.6 oz)	192	5
Kit Kat (1.5 oz)	230	12
Life Savers (.9 oz)	88	0
Peanut M & Ms (1.74 oz)	250	13
Mr. Goodbar (1.9 oz)	240	15
Sugar Daddy (2 oz)	218	1
Tootsie Roll (2.25 oz)	252	6
York Peppermint Patty (1.5 oz)	180	4

Women's Basketball

> **Suggested Activity:** With a partner, use the information provided below, to take turns asking and answering the following questions:

1. How tall is Ayanna Brown?
2. How tall is Megan Light?
3. How tall is Chanivia Broussard?
4. How tall is Holli Tapley?
5. How tall is Shelia James?
6. How tall is Amanda Papuga?
7. How tall is Schrene Isidora?
8. How tall is Alicia Hartlaub?
9. How tall is Gail Strumpf?
10. How tall is Meghan Saake?

Women's Basketball Players

Cardinal Starters	
Player	**Height**
Megan Light	5'6"
Holli Tapley	5'7"
Gail Strumpf	6'4"
Ayanna Brown	6'3"
Schrene Isidora	5'11"
Cougar Starters	
Player	**Height**
Amanda Papuga	5'10"
Sheila James	5'5"
Meghan Saake	5'10"
Alicia Hartlaub	6'2"
Chanivia Broussard	6'0"

Unit Ten: Fractions

- **Warm-Up Exercises**
- **Overview**
- **Activities:** **Food for Thought**
  Investor's Diary
  When in Rome, or Paris, or Rio . . .
  Telephone Game

Warm-Up Exercises

Shoulder Shrugs: Slowly raise and drop shoulders several times.

The Swan Dive: Slowly stretch arms above your head until they meet, palms together. Gently lower them to shoulder level, palms up. Repeat.

Finger Lifts: Place hand palm down on a table or flat surface and slowly raise and lower each finger. Repeat with the other hand.

Full Arm Stretch: Hold arm out parallel to the floor, palm down. Lock elbow. Raise your hand so the fingertips point to the ceiling. With the other hand, gently press the raised fingers back toward your body for a five-count. Alternate with the other hand. Repeat twice.

Palm Press: Press palms together in front of your body. Keeping your elbows high, use the right palm to gently and slowly push the left palm backwards, from the wrist only, toward the left elbow. Slowly and gently, use the left palm to push the right palm backwards, from the wrist only, toward the right elbow. Repeat several times.

The Frankenstein: With arms stretched out in front of you, palms down, slowly open and close hands, stretching the fingers apart as far as possible. Repeat several times.

Wrist Revolutions: With closed hands, slowly rotate wrists in toward each other several times. Then rotate wrists away from each other several times.

Overview

Fractions

The number in the numerator position is signed, followed by a slight downward motion while signing the number in thedenominator.

In fractions where both the numerator and denominator are single digits, the palm orientation for the entire fraction depends on the numerator. When the numerator is 1–5, both the numerator and denominator are signed palm in, even if the denominator contains a number greater than 5. However, when the numerator is 6–9, both the numerator and the denominator are signed palm out.

When the fraction is paired with a whole number, the fraction faces the same direction as the whole number. Thus, in $4^1/_2$, the fraction faces in, because the 4 faces in, but in $7^1/_2$, the fraction faces out.

Decimals

The decimal point in ASL is signed using the handshape of a boxed X.

Food for Thought

> **Suggested Activity:** With a partner, determine the serving size and calorie count for 2 servings of each item.

Rice Chex Serving Size 1¼ cup Servings per box 16 Calories per serving 120	Enriched Long Spaghetti Serving Size 2 oz Servings per box 11 Calories per serving 210
Wheat Thins Serving Size 16 crackers Servings per box 29 Calories per serving 150	Creamy Peanut Butter Serving Size 1¼ tbsp Servings per jar 16 Calories per serving 120
Blue Diamond Almonds Serving Size 3 tbsp Servings per can 11 Calories per serving 180	Bittersweet Swiss Chocolate Serving Size 12 squares Servings per bar 2.5 Calories per serving 210
Macaroni and Cheese Serving Size 2.5 oz Servings/container 3 Calories per serving 250	Salsa Serving Size 2 tbsp Servings/container 15 Calories per serving 10
Basil Rotini Tomato Soup Serving Size 1 cup Servings/container 2 Calories per serving 120	Sourdough Bread Serving Size 1 slice Servings/loaf 18 Calories per serving 100
Chopped Broccoli Serving Size ¾ cup Servings per box 3.5 Calories per serving 25	Pulp Free Orange Juice Serving Size 8 oz Servings per can 12 Calories per serving 110

Investor's Diary

> **Suggested Activity:** With a partner, use the information provided below to take turns asking and answering the following questions about stock prices:

1. What was the change for IBM?
2. What was the high for General Motors?
3. What was the low for Wal-Mart?
4. What was the high for Lucent?
5. What was the low for Disney?
6. What did BellSouth close at?
7. What was the change for Merck?
8. What did Exxon close at?
9. What was the high for AT&T?
10. What was the low for Microsoft?

Stock Prices

Stock	High	Low	Close	Change
AT&T	18.25	16.50	17.06	−1.88
BellSouth	41.06	39.72	40.13	−.81
Cisco	40.25	35.16	38.88	+2.38
Disney	27.69	26.50	27.69	+.63
Exxon	86.75	84.75	84.75	−.44
General Electric	48.50	47.19	47.88	+.44
General Motors	52.00	48.69	51.38	+1.38
IBM	87.94	80.06	81.56	−4.44
Lucent	14.56	12.50	14.19	−1.31
Merck	93.63	91.00	92.50	−.88
Microsoft	45.13	40.25	43.44	+1.94
Wal-Mart	52.25	49.31	51.75	+2.81

When in Rome, or Paris, or Rio...

> **Suggested Activity:** With a partner, use the U.S. dollar exchange rate chart for January 21, 2001 to ask and answer questions in the following form: How many *fingerspell currency* can I get for 1 U.S. dollar in *sign or fingerspell country?*

Example: How many *P-E-S-O-S* can I get for 1 US dollar in *A-R-G-E-N-T-I-N-A?*

Currency Exchange Rates (January 21, 2001)

1 U.S. Dollar equals	Currency	Country
0.97	Peso	Argentina
1.74	Dollar	Australia
1.86	Real	Brazil
0.65	Pound	Britain
1.45	Dollar	Canada
7.88	Yuan Renminbi	China, People's Republic of
7.69	Krone	Denmark
3.64	Pound	Egypt
7.49	Dollar	Hong Kong
3.09	New Shekel	Israel
114.00	Yen	Japan
74.76	Shilling	Kenya
9.39	New Peso	Mexico
2.16	Dollar	New Zealand
8.44	Kroner	Norway
51.52	Peso	Philippines
7.54	Rand	South Africa
1,216.00	Won	South Korea
9.17	Krona	Sweden
1.58	Franc	Switzerland
41.17	Baht	Thailand
673,780.00	Lira	Turkey
665.00	Bolivare	Venezuela

Telephone Game

> **Suggested Activity:** Divide into teams and form lines. The first person in each line faces the instructor; the rest turn around. The instructor signs one of the following items one time only to the front row of students. They then turn and tap the next person in line and sign the same number with context, until the last person has seen the number. That person comes to the front of the line and signs it back to the instructor. Teams with the correct number score one point.

6'3" tall

3:45 am

Social Security number: 311-72-5693

Phone number: (651) 483-1040

2,514 toothpicks

$4,554.99

$50.00 tickets to Rod Stewart

1965 Toyota Tercel

Daily Five Lotto: 8-10-60-25-12

Phone number: 824-9167

$1,489,311 lottery winnings

$1.50 admission

25,406 enrollment at Lansing Community College

¼ of an apple

67 goats

10:15 pm

25 pounds of lettuce

Daily Four Lotto: 5-29-63-22

½ of a pie

33% passed the test

Social Security number: 281-66-6222

2001 Honda Prelude

Zip Code 48864

5'11" tall

Record: 10 wins 3 loses

Unit Eleven: Ordinal Numbers

- **Warm-Up Exercises**
- **Overview**
- **Activities:** **Take Me out to the Ballgame**
  Peanuts & Crackerjacks
  Major League Baseball
  Let's Get Personal
  Out to Lunch
  Dewey Decimal Game

Warm-Up Exercises

Shoulder Shrugs: Slowly raise and drop shoulders several times.

The Swan Dive: Slowly stretch arms above your head until they meet, palms together. Gently lower them to shoulder level, palms up. Repeat.

Finger Lifts: Place hand palm down on a table or flat surface and slowly raise and lower each finger. Repeat with the other hand.

Full Arm Stretch: Hold arm out parallel to the floor, palm down. Lock elbow. Raise your hand so the fingertips point to the ceiling. With the other hand, gently press the raised fingers back toward your body for a five-count. Alternate with the other hand. Repeat twice.

Palm Press: Press palms together in front of your body. Keeping your elbows high, use the right palm to gently and slowly push the left palm backwards, from the wrist only, toward the left elbow. Slowly and gently, use the left palm to push the right palm backwards, from the wrist only, toward the right elbow. Repeat several times.

The Frankenstein: With arms stretched out in front of you, palms down, slowly open and close hands, stretching the fingers apart as far as possible. Repeat several times.

Wrist Revolutions: With closed hands, slowly rotate wrists in toward each other several times. Then rotate wrists away from each other several times.

Overview

Ordinal Numbers

Ordinal numbers have two applications: to show order (e.g., the first, second, and third steps in making a stained glass window) and to show position in a series of numbers (e.g., who came in first, second, and third in a race).

To show order, the number twists from palm out to palm in, the fingers remaining in an upright position throughout the movement.

To show position, the number starts palm out, in the regular upright position. The wrist then twists and pulls back toward the body, so the palm faces in, with the fingers rotating into a horizontal position, as shown in the following illustration.

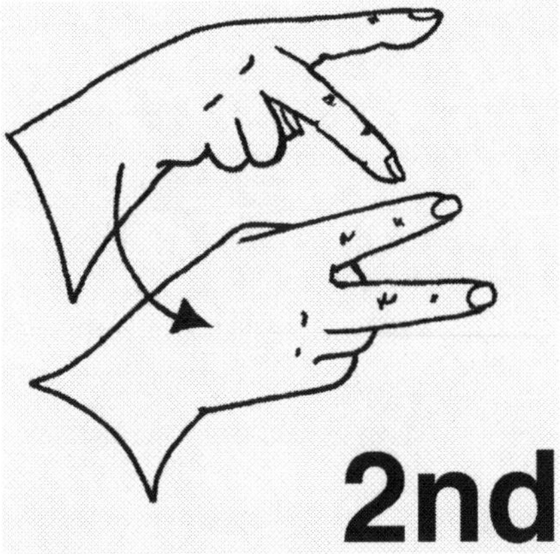

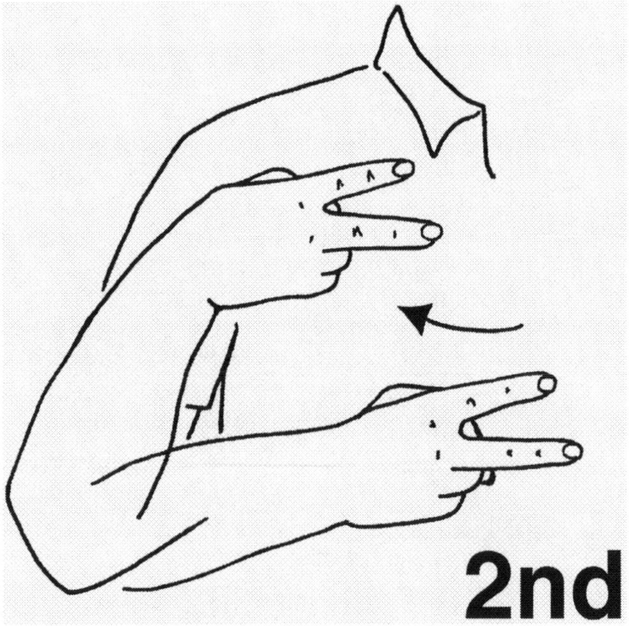

A variant to this second application would be a "throwing forward" of the number. "First," "second," and "third," etc. would be indicated by a sharp bounce of the number, palm left (for right-handed signers) in front of the body.

Take Me out to the Ballgame

> **Suggested Activity:** Using the information in the chart below, with a partner answer the win/loss standings questions for the teams below:

1. Identify, in order, the top five winning teams.
2. Identify, in order, the four teams with the worst records.
3. Identify, in order, the teams that have 90 or more wins.
4. Identify, in order, the teams that have 85 or more wins.
5. Identify, in order, the teams that have between 45 and 50 losses.

NATIONAL LEAGUE STANDINGS

EAST	Wins	Losses
Philadelphia	82	40
Atlanta	79	42
Florida	76	46
New York	63	58
Montreal	58	64
CENTRAL	**Wins**	**Losses**
Chicago	96	25
Houston	87	34
St. Louis	85	36
Milwaukee	78	44
Pittsburgh	77	45
Cincinnati	70	51
WEST	**Wins**	**Losses**
San Francisco	91	30
Arizona	89	32
Colorado	75	47
San Diego	69	52
Los Angeles	67	55

Peanuts & Crackerjacks

> **Suggested Activity:** With a partner, take turns asking and answering the following questions using the statistics below:

1. How many homeruns did the top hitter hit?
2. How many runs did Helton bat in?
3. How many strikeouts did Vazquez have?
4. What were Maddux's pitching wins/losses?
5. What are Sosa's homerun and RBI stats?

Baseball Statistics

Homeruns		Runs Batted In		Pitching Wins/Losses		Strikeouts	
Bonds	47	Gonzalez	106	Schilling	16-5	Johnson	259
Gonzalez	43	Sosa	101	Johnson	14-5	Schilling	205
Sosa	37	Helton	100	Lieber	14-5	Wood	183
Helton	34	Berkman	92	Maddux	14-6	Park	167
Green	31	Nevin	92	Morris	13-7	Vazquez	152
Nevin	31	Bagwell	91	Dempster	13-9	Burkett	143

Major League Baseball

> **Suggested Activity:** With a partner, use the statistics below to take turns asking and answering the following questions:

1. List in order, teams that had more than 2 million people attend home games.
2. List in order, teams that had 1.2 million people or less attend home games.
3. List in order, the top three teams for combined home and away attendance.
4. List in order, which four teams had the lowest combined home and away attendance.
5. List in order, teams that had combined home and away total attendance between 3,000,001 and 3,999,999

American League Attendance Report

Team	Home Attendance	Total Home and Away Attendance
Anaheim	1,320,125	3,196,916
Baltimore	2,092,256	3,634,013
Boston	1,888,478	3,572,461
Chicago	1,283,895	2,837,953
Cleveland	2,298,895	3,831,463
Detroit	1,406,921	2,915,100
Kansas City	1,055,978	2,756,206
Minnesota	1,303,717	2,962,003
New York	2,423,799	4,310,943
Oakland	1,330,651	2,970,778
Seattle	2,187,467	4,041,244
Tampa Bay	801,743	2,440,255
Texas	1,948,421	3,626,852
Toronto	1,390,479	2,788,371

Let's Get Personal

> **Suggested Activity:** With a partner, share the following numerical information (real or invented). Be sure to use appropriate ASL structure and grammatical features.

1. Couch Potato:
    - Number of hours of television watching per week?
    - How many channels you get?
    - Favorite channel?
    - Number of video rentals per year?

2. Employment:
    - Work schedule?
    - Length of your lunch break?
    - Office phone number?
    - Fax number?

3. School Days:
    - Age of your first crush?
    - Favorite grade in elementary school?
    - Cost of a hot lunch when you were in high school?
    - Time school started and ended?

4. Cars:
    - Age you got your first car?
    - How much did it cost?
    - Year of your current car?
    - How much did it cost?

Out to Lunch

> **Suggested Activity:** Divide into groups of three. Two students act as restaurant patrons, the third as their server. The patrons order from the menu below. The server writes down the ordered items, and then must calculate the final bill for the patrons. The patrons then calculate how much their total is, including a tip.

MENU

APPETIZERS		
	Soup of the Day	$3.50
	Fried Cheese	$4.25
	Blooming Onion	$4.75
	Cheese Breadsticks	$3.95
SALADS		
	House Salad	$3.25
	Caesar Salad	$5.25
	Grilled Chicken Salad	$7.59
	Cottage Cheese	$1.40
	Taco salad	$4.35
ENTREES		
	Spaghetti	$10.95
	With sausage or meatball	add $2.00
	Filet Mignon	$16.99
	Cheeseburger	$4.15
	Turkey Club	$4.75
	Pizza by the Slice (cheese only)	$1.95
	add .35 per topping	
DESSERTS		
	Apple Crisp	$4.99
	Hot Fudge Brownie Sundae	$4.95
	Cheesecake	$3.75
SIDES		
	French Fries	$1.50
	Onion Rings	$2.25
	Baked Potato	$2.00
	Rice	$1.50
	Vegetables	$1.50
BEVERAGES		
	Coffee, Tea (hot or iced)	$1.25
	Soft Drinks	$1.25
	Hot Chocolate	$1.50
	Espresso	$2.25
	Wine	$4.75

Dewey Decimal Game

> **Suggested Activity:** Divide into pairs. Each student takes a different list of Dewey Decimal System numbers for a variety of topics. Ask and answer the following questions using the tables below.

1. Where can I find books about the teachings of Zen?
2. Can I find information on tracing my family roots?
3. I need a cookbook.
4. How can I find out how to start a hog farm?
5. Can you show me a travel guide for Paris?
6. I need details about the fall of Rome.
7. Where are the books on George Washington Carver's life?
8. Where can I find information on early settlements in Australia?
9. I'm looking for my horoscope.
10. I need information on the early warning signs of a heart attack.

Dewey Decimal System

100	PHILOSOPHY	900	HISTORY
110	Metaphysics	910	Geography & travel
120	Epistimology	920	Biography & genealogy
130	Astrology, parapsychology & the occult	930	History of the ancient world (to ca. 499 A.D.)
140	Philosophical schools of thought	940	History of Europe (ca. 500 A.D. -)
150	Psychology	950	History of Asia
160	Logic	960	History of Africa
170	Ethics	970	History of North America
180	Ancient, Medieval, & Eastern philosophy	980	History of South America
190	Modern Western Philosophy	990	History of other regions

Dewey DecimalSystem—cont'd

600	**TECHNOLOGY**		
610	Medicine		
620	Engineering		
630	Agriculture		
640	Home & family management		
650	Management & public relations		
660	Chemical engineering		
670	Manufacturing		
680	Manufacturing specific products		
690	Building & construction		

Unit Twelve: Numbers in Sports

- Warm-Up Exercises
- Overview
- Activities: Sports Scores
  At the Track: Horse Racing
  Getting Creative
  Number Relay

Warm-Up Exercises

Shoulder Shrugs: Slowly raise and drop shoulders several times.

The Swan Dive: Slowly stretch arms above your head until they meet, palms together. Gently lower them to shoulder level, palms up. Repeat.

Finger Lifts: Place hand palm down on a table or flat surface and slowly raise and lower each finger. Repeat with the other hand.

Full Arm Stretch: Hold arm out parallel to the floor, palm down. Lock elbow. Raise your hand so the fingertips point to the ceiling. With the other hand, gently press the raised fingers back toward your body for a five-count. Alternate with the other hand. Repeat twice.

Palm Press: Press palms together in front of your body. Keeping your elbows high, use the right palm to gently and slowly push the left palm backwards, from the wrist only, toward the left elbow. Slowly and gently, use the left palm to push the right palm backwards, from the wrist only, toward the right elbow. Repeat several times.

The Frankenstein: With arms stretched out in front of you, palms down, slowly open and close hands, stretching the fingers apart as far as possible. Repeat several times.

Wrist Revolutions: With closed hands, slowly rotate wrists in toward each other several times. Then rotate wrists away from each other several times.

Overview

Numbers in Sports

Jersey/player numbers are signed palm out close to the chest.

Jersey Number 99

Sport scores are signed by indicating the winning score first. This can be done by signing the winning score with one hand, followed by the losing score with the other. It can also be done by using the same hand, starting with the winning score close to the body and the losing score away from the body.

"Home team" (or "my/our" team) and "Away team" (or "their" team) also can be indicated with the close-to-the-body/away-from-the-body movements. The home team score can be signed with one hand, followed by the away team score with the other. You can also do this with two hands, starting with the home team score close to the body and the away team score away from the body.

If the game ends in a tie, both hands are used, signing the score simultaneously while moving from the center of the sign space (close to the body) to opposite sides (right and left).

Sports Scores

> **Suggested Activity:** With a partner, take turns giving the following scores (including team names), as if you are a NEUTRAL observer.

Basketball

Jazz	99	Suns	98
Lakers	104	Raptors	101
Pistons	102	Hornets	97
Pacers	89	Magic	84
Sixers	103	Clippers	92
Bulls	96	Nuggets	93
Celtics	100	Cavaliers	95
Warriors	92	Spurs	88

> **Suggested Activity:** With a partner take turns giving the following scores (including team names), as if you (the signer) are on the WINNING team.

Girls Soccer

St. Thomas Aquinas	9	Miami Lourdes	0
American Heritage	4	Bishop Verot	1
Douglas	5	Spruce Creek	3
Astronautville	6	Cardinal Gibbons	2
Key West	2	Travella	2
Westminster Academy	7	Coconut Creek	4

> **Suggested Activity:** With a partner take turns giving the following scores (including team names), as if you (the signer) are on the LOSING team.

Boys Hockey

Grand Ledge	4	Saugatuck	0
Williamston	5	Owosso	3
Portland	4	Dansville	3
Lansing	3	Charlotte	3
Mason	3	Holt	2
Eaton Rapids	1	Okemos	1

At the Track: Horse Racing

> **Suggested Activity:** With a partner, use the information provided below to take turns asking and answering the following questions. Use ordinals (first, second, third, etc.) in your answers.

1. If the horses won based on alphabetical order, which horses would win, place, and show?
2. List in order the four lightest jockeys and their weights.
3. List in order the five heaviest jockeys and their weights.
4. List, in alphabetical order, jockeys who weigh 117 or 118 pounds.
5. List, in alphabetical order, jockeys who ride a horse with "Glitter" in its name.

Horses and Jockeys

Horse	Jockey	Weight (lbs.)
Circle's Wish	Coa	113
Burnham	Nunez	121
Well Designed	Douglas	114
Lady Glitter	Sukar	122
All Best Wishes	Garcia	120
Glitter Miss	Castellano	123
Zanny's Dancer	Toribio	117
Dixie Special	Rivera II	119
True Glitter	Alcoa	110
Nautical Nellie	Carlo	118
Sweetest Secret	Chavez	115
Shady Lane	Douglas	118
Bitter Bride	Velez	112
Carson City Girl	Aguirre	111

Getting Creative

> **Suggested Activity:** Create a story to sign for your class incorporating the following numeric topics.

1. Race Announcement:
   - Distance of the run
   - Time the race starts
   - Age group you are in
   - First prize

2. Sports Update:
   - Dates of basketball tournament
   - Jersey number of your favorite player
   - Height of the center
   - Final Score

3. Soccer Program:
   - Number of kids on the team
   - Cost per family
   - Games won-lost-tied
   - Number of teams in the league

4. Girls Basketball:
   - Time the game starts
   - Cost of admission
   - Score at half time
   - Final score

Number Relay

> **Suggested Activity:** Divide into teams and form lines. The first person in each line goes to the blackboard ready to write. The instructor picks a number from the list below and signs it. The first student to correctly write the number on the board wins a point for their team. Students then pass the chalk to the next student in line and go to the back of the line.

5'9" tall

1,301 marbles in a jar

765 fish in a tank

300 sheep

87 plants

25 people

99¢ hamburgers

Social Security number: 812-33-3678

7:23 am

Daily Four Lotto: 12-25-9-33

4½ feet

$8.00 book

1999 VW Bug

50% of people drive black cars

15,681 people at a conference

1:00 pm

Social Security number: 310-29-6776

Phone Number: 930-3225

Daily Three Lotto: 27-16-3

21 years old

6,708,504 condos in New York City

½ inch thickness of a piece of wood

$10,000,000 lottery

6'2" tall

Record: 12 wins 10 losses

Score: 59 to 33

Appendix A

Numbers 0–10 Illustrations

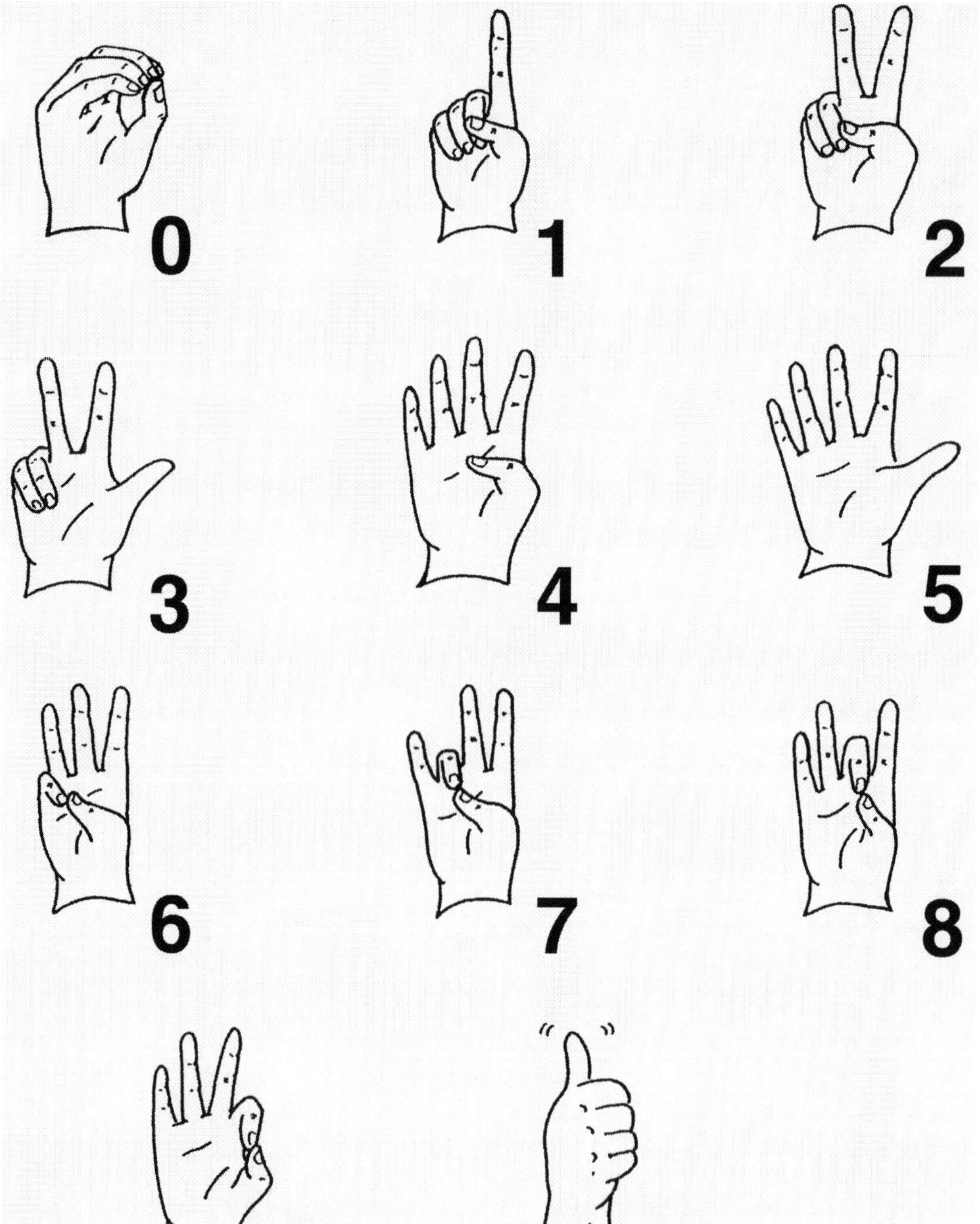

Numbers 1–10 Illustrations

1

2

3

4

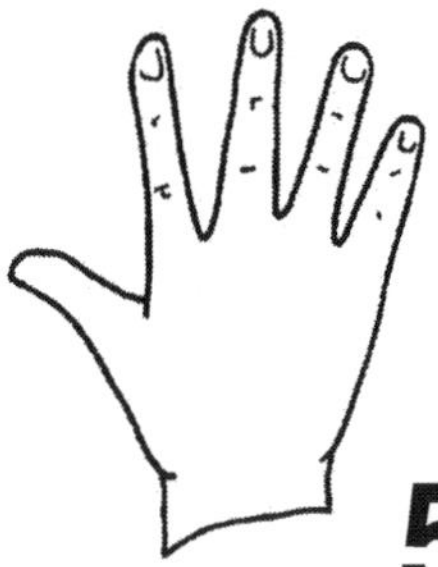
5

6

7

8

9

10

Bibliography and Resource List

Bahleda, S. (1996). *Fingerspelling the Real World.* Eagle River, AK: Real World Press.

Cardinal and Ordinal Systems [videotape]. (1989). Burtonsville, MD: Sign Media, Inc.

Fingerspelling and Numbers [computer software]. (1994). Salem, OR: Sign Enhancers, Inc.

Incorporating Systems [videotape]. (1989). Burtonsville, MD: Sign Media, Inc.

Interactive Sign Language Fingerspelling and Numbers [computer software]. (1997). Seattle: Palatine, Inc.

Number Signs for Everyone: Numbering in American Sign Language [videotape]. (1997). San Diego: Dawn Sign Press.

Numbering in American Sign Language: Number Signs for Everyone. (1998). San Diego: Dawn Sign Press.

Unique Systems [videotape]. (1989). Burtonsville, MD: Sign Media, Inc.

Made in the USA
Las Vegas, NV
22 January 2024

84751066R00070